THE PRODIGAL SPOUSE

A CHRISTIAN'S GUIDE TO MARRIAGE

THE PRODIGAL SPOUSE

A CHRISTIAN'S GUIDE TO MARRIAGE

~ †✝† ~

JUDGE HAL MOROZ

PREFACE BY

PAUL & VICKIE HAFER

MINISTERS OF THE GOSPEL
& RADIO SHOW HOSTS
AT THE LIGHTHOUSE WECC
CHRISTIAN RADIO STATION

NEW YORK   ATLANTA   WASHINGTON   MEXICO CITY   JERUSALEM

The Prodigal Spouse:
A Christian's Guide to Marriage
Judge Hal Moroz

Special Thanks to Paul and Vickie Hafer of Lighthouse Christian Broadcasting,
The Lighthouse WECC 89.3 FM Christian Radio Ministry,
5465 Hwy 40 E, St. Marys, GA 31558
912-882-8930, http://www.thelighthousefm.org

Unless otherwise noted, Scripture quotations are from
The King James Version of the Bible.

Scripture taken from the New King James Version®.
Copyright © 1982 by Thomas Nelson, Inc.
Used by permission. All rights reserved.

The text of the New King James Version® (NKJV®) may be quoted or reprinted without prior written permission with the following qualifications: (1) up to and including 1,000 verses may be quoted in printed form so long as the verses quoted amount to less than 50% of a complete book of the Bible and make up less than 50% of the total work in which they are quoted; (2) all NKJV quotations must conform accurately to the NKJV text.

For quotation requests not covered by the above guidelines, write to
Thomas Nelson, Inc., Attention: Bible Rights and Permissions,
P.O. Box 141000, Nashville, TN 37214-1000.

Scripture taken from the NEW AMERICAN STANDARD BIBLE®,
Copyright © 1960,1962,1963,1968,1971,1972,1973,1975,1977,1995
by The Lockman Foundation. Used by Permission.

The opinions expressed in this book are solely the opinions of the author and do not necessarily reflect the opinions of any individual, groups, organizations or business entities mentioned herein.
The quotes, selected writings, and articles contained in this book are reprinted with permission or are permissible for use under existing law.

Printed in the United States of America

The Prodigal Spouse

A Christian's Guide to Marriage

If there is one great Truth to be gleamed from this work,
it is this …

Your thoughts become your attitude, your words,
and your deeds. Where the mind goes, the man follows.

Satan seeks to defeat You by tempting You
to trust in your own wisdom.

TRUST IN GOD!

This work is dedicated to the Glory of God

~*~

*"Let your light so shine before men, that they may see your good
works, and glorify your Father which is in heaven."*

~ Matthew 5:16

The Prodigal Spouse

A Christian's Guide to Marriage

Judge Hal Moroz

Contents

"⁶ Therefore hath the curse devoured the earth,
and they that dwell therein are desolate:
therefore the inhabitants of the earth are burned, and few men left.
⁷ The new wine mourneth, the vine languisheth,
all the merryhearted do sigh.
⁸ The mirth of tabrets ceaseth, the noise of them that rejoice endeth,
the joy of the harp ceaseth.
⁹ They shall not drink wine with a song;
strong drink shall be bitter to them that drink it.
¹⁰ The city of confusion is broken down:
every house is shut up, that no man may come in.
¹¹ There is a crying for wine in the streets; all joy is darkened,
the mirth of the land is gone.
¹² In the city is left desolation, and the gate is smitten with destruction."

~ Isaiah 24:6-12

Preface

Marriage Takes Three

"To paraphrase 2 Peter 1:21, 'Holy men of old spoke as God the Holy Spirit moved them.' And Hebrew 13:8 tells us, 'Jesus Christ is the same yesterday, and today, and forever.' And so today, God speaks to men and women, and I can think of no better words of wisdom from outside the pages of the Bible, consistent with the message of the Bible, that speak to us about the topic of Marriage, than from my friends and family in Christ, Paul and Vickie Hafer.

It is my prayer these words of Paul and Vickie Hafer will be a blessing to you as we begin this parable of The Prodigal Spouse."

~ Hal Moroz

From Paul:

During a discussion on marriage, I recall hearing someone say, "Getting married is easy; staying married is the challenge!" I believe there is a small measure of reality in that observation. There are challenges throughout life, but the truth is, remaining married is not one of them! To the contrary, being joined in the covenant of holy matrimony makes the husband and wife better equipped, to face and handle any of life's challenges, while also enjoying the gift of life together.

My wife Vickie and I consider ourselves blessed and very fortunate to share life and love as husband and wife, as parents to our daughter, grandparents to three adorable grandkids, and to share in ministry together on The Lighthouse WECC.

As we approach our 40th wedding anniversary this month, we thank God today for the joy and rewards of married life, as much as we did 40 years ago when He joined us in a covenant union with each other. And we thank Him every day for sustaining it on a strong foundation. A foundation of being best friends (we always preferred to be with each other more than anyone else, and we <u>are</u>, pretty much, 24 hours a day!). A foundation of shared interest in the things of life. A foundation of mutual respect and honor for each other. And a faith foundation that God brought us together, to become one!

On occasions when we're privileged to officiate a wedding, we always point out that when two born-again believers come before God to be united as husband and wife, the two are uniting to become one, and the Apostle Paul calls this new "one" a mystery, but it's a mystery that serves as an illustration of how Christ and the Church are also one.

Far too often when couples join as husband and wife, they don't catch the vision of being "one," but rather as two people in a legal agreement that can be dissolved at any time. In marriage we are of course joined in a legal contract, but far more important, we're joined in a spiritual union, a sacred contract before God, exchanging vows to become one in a covenant of love.

We never consider marriage to be an agreement that must be endured because of the vows of commitment and contractual obligations, striving to suffer thru the "challenges" of life as a married couple, but rather, as a great privilege and joy to share life's journey together, such that a greater challenge would be to go thru life alone. We know that single believers, or widows, certainly enjoy life as well with the ever-present Christ who gives us purpose, and a hope-filled future, but the institution of marriage is ordained by God to provide a special joy for husband and wife together.

Our marriage has remained strong because the foundation continues to be strengthened. We're still best friends, we still lovingly share (and sometimes pretend to share) all the same interests, and we still share and pray together in faith to our God who brought us together.

In this book, Hal Moroz, our dear friend and brother in Christ, has exposed the tools of Satan and every weapon of hell that he uses to destroy a marriage. But more importantly, he reveals the foundational and scriptural tools God has provided to equip every husband and wife to preserve and strengthen the bonds of love in holy matrimony, and, for *The Prodigal Spouse* to return to the love of the covenant vows.

From Vickie:

I was the "Prodigal Wife"... Not once, but twice. As Paul so beautifully stated, we are celebrating our 40th Anniversary. God has blessed me with the most amazing husband. He took this prodigal, this broken, insecure girl and because of His great love, grace, and mercy, blessed me beyond measure. He is the God of second, third, AND beyond chances! Let this book be an encouragement to never give up. We serve a God of miracles!

"Marriage Takes Three"

I once thought marriage took
Just two to make a go.
But now I am convinced
It takes the Lord also.

And not one marriage fails
When Christ is asked to enter.
As lovers come together
With Jesus at the center.

But marriage seldom thrives
And homes are incomplete
Till He is welcomed there
To help avert defeat

In Homes where Christ is first
It's obvious to see.
Those unions really work.
For Marriage still takes three.

Paul gave me this poem on our first Christmas as husband and wife. He was fully devoted to Christ and was confident that his new wife (me) would realize that with Christ, our marriage would be blessed and NOT FAIL. 40 years later, Christ remains in the center of our marriage.

Our prayer for you as you read *The Prodigal Spouse* is that you too will make Christ the center in every aspect of your marriage. Today is a new day to Begin Again! God is Forever Faithful!

Vickie & Paul Hafer

~~~~~~~~~~

"Arise, shine; for thy light is come,
and the glory of the LORD is risen upon thee.

For, behold, the darkness shall cover the earth,
and gross darkness the people: but the LORD shall arise upon thee,
and his glory shall be seen upon thee."

~ Isaiah 60:1-2

Introduction

To Know God is to Trust God

*"That your faith should not stand in the wisdom of men,
but in the power of God."*

~ 1 Corinthians 2:5

The inspiration for writing this book came to me in the midst of a personal crisis. I reached out to friends, actually saints, Paul and Vickie Hafer, for their wise, godly counsel and support. I knew that there was a lesson in my tribulation, a lesson that needed to be shared, about understanding and combating an evil in our time that has permeated our legal system and our families. That evil is Divorce and those who promote such an abomination, and I do not use those words lightly.

I shared my thoughts about this book, and Vickie responded by telling me, *"Start with your testimony and your stance ALWAYS against divorce. And NEVER agreeing to represent anyone in a divorce."* And so I shall.

I am a Christian and an American. I was born in poverty. My father was a World War II veteran, and served in the United States Navy. The ship he was on in the South Pacific during the war was torpedoed by the Japanese, but he survived on a raft with other sailors having engaged the Japanese in a battle as sea. He returned to America, met his future wife, my mother, and he labored as a longshoreman on the docks in Brooklyn, New York, and provided for his family. He was born the same year as President Kennedy, and died the same year as well. I was only 5 years old when he died, but I knew him. His name was Henry.

My mother was a housewife, never graduated high school, but set my feet on the path of knowledge and a relationship with God. She was a religious woman, and she loved me unconditionally. Her name was Helen.

I was born in America, during the time of Eisenhower's presidency, and America was comprised of 48 states. Vietnam was on the horizon, and the specter of American youth serving a cause greater than self always had a profound impact on my life. I joined the military at seventeen, and never looked back. I credit my military service with a great many things in my life. I learned discipline and setting priorities, went to college, military schooling, and even afterwards law school, which seemed like a logical transition, with all the rules and regulations.

As a Second Lieutenant in the United States Army, I married, was blessed with children, and privileged to have a wife that shared the Gospel with my children, even when I was not receptive to that voice. I wish now I could have shook some sense into the young, insecure man I was, who relied on my own power to control the destiny of my life and others. I had no anchor in God or His immovable, unshakeable Word. I relied on my own wisdom. I was wrong, and still regret it.

The bottom line is that I do see the necessity for a book such as this, if for no other reason than to shed light on the cultural war that rages in our society, and the Truth that needs to be told and shared and lived.

I eventually became a lawyer, a judge, a teacher, and a state prosecutor, but no venture was greater than discovering a relationship with Jesus Christ, which I had not done through most of my life. I knew God. I even witnessed His hand in my life and that of my family, but I did not have a personal relationship with Him. And thankfully, that all changed, not by my works, but by His grace. I was so blessed to hear the voice of the Holy Spirit through my wife, Dr. Jerry Falwell, Paul and Vickie Hafer, Dr. Charles Stanley, and a legion of saints unaware. I am proof that the Word does not return void.[1]

While it may not ingratiate me to a large bulk of the legal profession, I do NOT hold so-called *"Divorce Attorneys"* in high regard. Nor do I believe their practice comports to the express words of Jesus Christ or the Bible as a whole. *"What therefore God hath joined together, let not man put asunder."*[2] In fact, they are diametrically opposed to the fundamental precepts of Western Civilization and the teachings of Christ and the notion of being a Christian, or a follower of Christ. And I will argue that throughout this work, and all I would hope is that the reader would objectively consider my arguments and authorities.

As Vickie Hafer and others know, I would NEVER represent anyone in a Divorce proceeding. I stand AGAINST this plague called Divorce and the proponents of it. I would sooner starve than make a penny off of this heresy. As Jesus said in Matthew 5:30, *"And if thy right hand offend thee, cut it off, and cast it from thee: for it is profitable for thee that one of thy members should perish, and not that thy whole body should be cast*

---

[1] Isaiah 55:11: *"So shall my word be that goeth forth out of my mouth: it shall not return unto me void, but it shall accomplish that which I please, and it shall prosper in the thing whereto I sent it."*
[2] Mark 10:9.

into hell."

The institution of Marriage is a primary target of Satan, and that must be understood to overcome the fiery darts of the Devil and his demons. And the Devil and his demons exist, and I have witnessed them at work.

Marriage is a blessing and a time-honored union between a man and a woman. It is something to be treasured, and NEVER abandoned or tried before men to be divided and put asunder for the false promise of a *"better life."* It is spoken of in the Bible. It is a covenant between two adults, a man and a woman, and God. The man and the woman take vows of marriage before God and men. And those vows, like the one I had taken as a soldier, are inviolate. And it needs to be understood that vows are NOT taken for the good times in life, but they are taken specifically for the bad times, the times of tribulation, the times of sickness, the so-called *"worse"* times. That is when the measure of a person is taken. I am reminded during these times of the words of Charles Spurgeon, *"Never doubt in the darkness what God has shown you in the light."* Our character and the true measure of our relationship with God is taken when those vows are tested.

And it is my hope that this book will help You stand when that time comes, and it will come ...

~~~~~~~~~~

"Trust in the LORD with all thine heart;
and lean not unto thine own understanding.
In all thy ways acknowledge him, and he shall direct thy paths."

~ Proverbs 3:5-6

Chapter 1

The Prodigal

"'For I know the plans that I have for you,' declares the Lord,
'plans for welfare and not for calamity to give you a future and a hope.'"

~ Jeremiah 29:11

"And we know that all things work together for good to them that love God,
to them who are the called according to his purpose."

~ Romans 8:28

The Parable of the Prodigal Son is found in the text of the New Testament, in Luke 15:11-32 to be exact. It was told by Jesus to His followers to illustrate God's love and forgiveness, even when one would abandon the security and blessings God has bestowed, to follow a fallen *"wisdom"* over that which God has provided. It is illustrative of a common theme woven throughout the Bible, starting with Adam and Eve, through the Tower of Babel, to the doubting Israelites in the wilderness ... and even to the present day.

The truth of the Parable of the Prodigal Son applies to spouses as well, and it is a testament to God's unconditional love and the realization that our loved ones will sometimes head out on their own, outside the will of God, only to realize the treasure they lost in their rebellion. And it bears noting that in the Parable of the Prodigal Son, the father had the means and wherewithal to stop his son from leaving, but knew it was the choice of his son. And the Parable is a lesson in the ways God works, and those ways are explored throughout this work.

This is the timeless Parable of the Prodigal Son found in the Book of Luke, Chapter 15:

[11] And he said, A certain man had two sons:

[12] And the younger of them said to his father, Father, give me the portion of goods that falleth to me. And he divided unto them his living.

[13] And not many days after the younger son gathered all together, and took his journey into a far country, and there wasted his substance with riotous living.

[14] And when he had spent all, there arose a mighty famine in that land; and he began to be in want.

[15] And he went and joined himself to a citizen of that country; and he sent him into his fields to feed swine.

[16] And he would fain have filled his belly with the husks that the swine did eat: and no man gave unto him.

[17] And when he came to himself, he said, How many hired servants of my father's have bread enough and to spare, and I perish with hunger!

[18] I will arise and go to my father, and will say unto him, Father, I have sinned against heaven, and before thee,

[19] And am no more worthy to be called thy son: make me as one of thy hired servants.

[20] And he arose, and came to his father. But when he was yet a great way off, his father saw him, and had compassion, and ran, and fell on his neck, and kissed him.

[21] And the son said unto him, Father, I have sinned against heaven, and in thy sight, and am no more worthy to be called thy son.

[22] But the father said to his servants, Bring forth the best robe, and put it on him; and put a ring on his hand, and shoes on his feet:

[23] And bring hither the fatted calf, and kill it; and let us eat, and be merry:

[24] For this my son was dead, and is alive again; he was lost, and is found. And they began to be merry.

[25] Now his elder son was in the field: and as he came and drew nigh to the house, he heard musick and dancing.

[26] And he called one of the servants, and asked what these things meant.

[27] And he said unto him, Thy brother is come; and thy father hath killed the fatted calf, because he hath received him safe and sound.

[28] And he was angry, and would not go in: therefore came his father out, and intreated him.

[29] And he answering said to his father, Lo, these many years do I serve thee, neither

transgressed I at any time thy commandment: and yet thou never gavest me a kid, that I might make merry with my friends:

30 But as soon as this thy son was come, which hath devoured thy living with harlots, thou hast killed for him the fatted calf.

31 And he said unto him, Son, thou art ever with me, and all that I have is thine.

32 It was meet that we should make merry, and be glad: for this thy brother was dead, and is alive again; and was lost, and is found.

This is the Parable of the Prodigal Son, and its principles and lessons are applicable to all, but in the context of this book, it is applicable to the institution of marriage and those who would partake in such vows, especially *The Prodigal Spouse.*

~~~~~~~~~~

"You will turn back to me and ask for help, and I will answer your prayers."

~ Jeremiah 29:12

Chapter 2

Marriage

"Love beareth all things, believeth all things,
hopeth all things, endureth all things.

~ 1 Corinthians 13:7

Marriage is sacred! This fact must be fundamentally understood in any discussion of the subject. It is, according to Holy Scripture, a covenant created by God,[3] two people that *"God hath joined together."*[4] It is the union of one man with one woman, by and with Almighty God. It is one of the profoundest creations of God at the foundation of the world. And it was at that time, following the creation of man, in Genesis 2:18, we learn, *"And the LORD God said, It is not good that the man should be alone; I will make him an help meet for him."* This brought forth God's creation of the woman and wife, and God shared the model of this covenant when He said in Genesis 2:24, *"Therefore shall a man leave his father and his mother, and shall cleave unto his wife: and they shall be one flesh."* One man, one woman, united together with God. This is the Covenant of Marriage.

So there is no doubt, God considers Marriage important.

---

[3] Genesis 2:7, 22.
[4] Mark 10:9.

So much so, that Marriage is spoken of throughout the Old Testament,[5] as well as the New.[6] Jesus even began His many miracles at a marriage in Cana of Galilee,[7] where He turned water into wine, and as Holy Scripture tells us, He *"manifested forth his glory; and his disciples believed on Him."*[8] And Jesus himself spoke of Marriage as an unbreakable covenant when He said in Mark 10:9, *"What therefore God hath joined together, let not man put asunder."* If Marriage is that important to God, then it should be important to us!

And it deserves noting that marriage brings forth blessings. It is a cure for loneliness,[9] help in time of need,[10] a source of exhortation,[11] and the discovery of a best friend. And Proverbs 18:22 tells us, *"Whoso findeth a wife findeth a good thing, and obtaineth favour of the Lord."* Marriage is a great blessing!

Remember this: Marriage is miraculous! Holy Scripture tells us a married couple is *"one flesh."*[12] This is a creation of God. Positive and frequent communications are key to building upon this godly relationship. And if you are married, this communication is with God and your spouse. And on this point, I make the following two comments.

(1) Your spouse is supposed to be your best friend, next to the Lord. Treat them with respect and deference.

---

[5] Genesis 34:9; Exodus 21:10; Deuteronomy 7:3; Joshua 23:12; Psalm 78:63.

[6] Matthew 22:2; Matthew 22:4; Matthew 22:9; Matthew 22:30; Matthew 24:38; Matthew 25:10; Mark 12:25; Luke 17:27; Luke 20:34; Luke 20:35; John 2:1; John 2:2; 1 Corinthians 7:38; Hebrews 13:4; Revelation 19:7; Revelation 19:9.

[7] John 2:1-11.

[8] John 2:11.

[9] Genesis 2:18.

[10] Ibid.

[11] Hebrews 10:25.

[12] Genesis 2:24; Mark 10:8.

When a spouse disagrees with you, do not react as if you are under attack. Do not render evil. Take it as a constructive opinion. It may be a valid opinion, or it may not. The point is to listen with kindness and gentleness, as these are fruit of the Spirit, knowing that all comments made to you are coming from a person who loves you and has your best interests at heart. This is being godly and giving a blessing to your best friend.

(2) In this book, I strongly encourage prayer. God commands it![13] So pray! Pray that your words to your spouse are edifying and pleasing to God. Ask God to make you the person He desires you to be in your marriage. Demonstrate faith, hope and love. Share these prayers and desires of your heart with your spouse. Let your spouse know of your ongoing commitment to do the will of God, which is to be joyful in marriage and to be the person and spouse conformed to the image of Christ. Communicate together in prayer to God. It is an amazing experience!

With all of this said, I have also heard friends happily married lament certain passages of Scripture, such as Mark 12:25 [*"For when they shall rise from the dead, they neither marry, nor are given in marriage; but are as the angels which are in heaven."*] and Matthew 22:30 [*"For in the resurrection they neither marry, nor are given in marriage, but are as the angels of*

---

13 1 Thessalonians 5:17.

God in heaven."] The implication here is that marriages will no longer exist in the second coming or in heaven, and we might somehow lose our best friend.

In this perceived dilemma, we need to realize the Gospel is always Good News to the believer. I say this because we need to view these passages in context. Matthew 22:30 simply states that *"in the resurrection they neither marry, nor are given in marriage."* That literally means there will be no more marriages in the afterlife. There is no mention of us losing our spouses in heaven, or a breaking of the marriage covenant once we die. Scripture says we will be *"as the angels"*[14] of God in heaven. And 1 John 3:2 provides us the great hope and reassurance that we will be even closer to our spouses in heaven, *"Beloved, now are we the sons of God, and it doth not yet appear what we shall be: but we know that, when He shall appear, we shall be like Him; for we shall see Him as He is."* Note, *"we shall be like Him,"*[15] which means having greater love than we could ever have as human beings. We will have His unconditional, irrevocable love, and that love will be for our Lord as well as our spouse. No union could be greater! It is a powerful testimony!

However, despite the magnificent beauty of the marriage covenant, we find in legal parlance that marriage is nothing more than a mere *"contract."* A contract is a legal instrument whereby one person makes an *"offer,"* another *"accepts"* the offer, and *"consideration"* is made. And being a contract, it can be broken, breached, modified, or enforced, depending upon a person's feelings or desires at the movement. Contracts can be made between any adults and/or businesses, provided they have the capacity to enter into one,

[14] Mark 12:25 & Matthew 22:30.
[15] 1 John 3:2.

and it is not made under duress. But there is a bright line distinction between contracts and biblical covenants. Contracts are man-made, but biblical covenants are made by God, and in this respect marriages are unique and very special.

In the *"wisdom"* of modern men, and particularly the architects of Divorce, we are led to believe marriage is harmful, the thought of being *"co-dependent"* is abhorrent and to be avoided at all costs. We also witness this rhetoric in the *"justification"* of murdering babies in their mothers wombs, or even after these babies survive botched abortion attempts, and are left to die alone in abortion clinic closets or garbage cans. They call evil good, and good evil.[16] And remember what Jesus said about such men [and women] in John 8:44: *"Ye are of your father the devil, and the lusts of your father ye will do. He was a murderer from the beginning, and abode not in the truth, because there is no truth in him. When he speaketh a lie, he speaketh of his own: for he is a liar, and the father of it."*

And I understand there are present-day activists who desire to outlaw such speech, attempting to make it a *"hate crime"* or punishable offense to utter such Godly truth, and they do this all in the misguided notion of being *"Politically Correct"* or *"tolerant"* of the sensitivities of others, all to the exclusion of our God-given Constitutional rights to Free Speech and Freedom of Religion.

Ending marriages in divorce, breaking covenants with God because of occasional feelings and seasons of discontent, forsaking your spouse for any reason, redefining marriage

---

[16] Isaiah 5:20: *"Woe unto them that call evil good, and good evil; that put darkness for light, and light for darkness; that put bitter for sweet, and sweet for bitter!"*

because it is popular to do so or politically in fashion, are never the way to go. They are abominations, and many have fallen for this heresy. Leviticus 18:22-30 reveals the harsh truths and the consequences of such abominations to the offender and their nation:

> 22 Thou shalt not lie with mankind, as with womankind: it is abomination.

> 23 Neither shalt thou lie with any beast to defile thyself therewith: neither shall any woman stand before a beast to lie down thereto: it is confusion.

> 24 Defile not ye yourselves in any of these things: for in all these the nations are defiled which I cast out before you:

> 25 And the land is defiled: therefore I do visit the iniquity thereof upon it, and the land itself vomiteth out her inhabitants.

> 26 Ye shall therefore keep my statutes and my judgments, and shall not commit any of these abominations; neither any of your own nation, nor any stranger that sojourneth among you:

> 27 (For all these abominations have the men of the land done, which were before you, and the land is defiled;)

> 28 That the land spue not you out also, when ye defile it, as it spued out the nations that were before you.

> 29 For whosoever shall commit any of these abominations, even the souls that commit them shall be cut off from among their people.

30 Therefore shall ye keep mine ordinance, that ye commit not any one of these abominable customs, which were committed before you, and that ye defile not yourselves therein: I am the LORD your God.

Furthermore, Isaiah 5:20 cautions, *"Woe unto them that call evil good, and good evil; that put darkness for light, and light for darkness; that put bitter for sweet, and sweet for bitter!"* These practices are not consistent with the Word of God, and because they are not, we learn of the consequences of such behavior in Romans 1:18-32:

18 For the wrath of God is revealed from heaven against all ungodliness and unrighteousness of men, who hold the truth in unrighteousness;

19 Because that which may be known of God is manifest in them; for God hath shewed it unto them.

20 For the invisible things of him from the creation of the world are clearly seen, being understood by the things that are made, even his eternal power and Godhead; so that they are without excuse:

21 Because that, when they knew God, they glorified him not as God, neither were thankful; but became vain in their imaginations, and their foolish heart was darkened.

22 Professing themselves to be wise, they became fools,

23 And changed the glory of the uncorruptible God into an image made like to corruptible man, and to birds, and fourfooted beasts, and creeping things.

24 Wherefore God also gave them up to uncleanness through the lusts of their own hearts, to dishonour their own bodies between themselves:

25 Who changed the truth of God into a lie, and worshipped and served the creature more than the Creator, who is blessed for ever. Amen.

26 For this cause God gave them up unto vile affections: for even their women did change the natural use into that which is against nature:

27 And likewise also the men, leaving the natural use of the woman, burned in their lust one toward another; men with men working that which is unseemly, and receiving in themselves that recompence of their error which was meet.

28 And even as they did not like to retain God in their knowledge, God gave them over to a reprobate mind, to do those things which are not convenient;

29 Being filled with all unrighteousness, fornication, wickedness, covetousness, maliciousness; full of envy, murder, debate, deceit, malignity; whisperers,

30 Backbiters, haters of God, despiteful, proud, boasters, inventors of evil things, disobedient to parents,

31   Without   understanding, covenantbreakers,   without   natural affection, implacable, unmerciful:

32 Who knowing the judgment of God, that they which commit such things are worthy of death, not only do the same, but have pleasure in them that do them.

These are the harsh consequences of disobedience. It is what happens when we ignore the Word of God and call something evil *"good,"* and something good *"evil."* Breaking covenants is never the way to success or positive personal growth. The Bible is replete with such examples. Doesn't it make sense to obey God, reap the blessings, and leave the consequences to Him?

In my own walk, I have heard many rationalize their behavior. They argue from personal desire, not seeing things as God sees them. They see things from their own eyes. We hear, *"well, even Jesus said divorce is permitted."* Did He? They often cite Matthew 19:9 out of context, when Jesus said, *"Whosoever shall put away his wife, except it be for fornication, and shall marry another, committeth adultery: and whoso marrieth her which is put away doth commit adultery."* People narrowly interpret this to mean divorce is permitted when one spouse is engaged in an adulterous relationship, but they are wrong. Jesus was citing a precept of Moses because of the hardness of peoples' hearts. People who rationalize divorce fail to cite the previous verse, Matthew 19:8, where Jesus said unto them, *"Moses because of the hardness of your hearts suffered you to put away your wives: but from the beginning it was not so."* And in this same conversation with the Pharisees in Mark 10:5, Jesus said of Moses, *"For the hardness of your heart he wrote you this precept."* Jesus was talking about how the hardness of hearts turned men from the Word of God, and how divorce was a *"precept"* of man, not a commandment of God. It is particularly noteworthy that Jesus said, *"but from the beginning it was not so."*[17] Remember, if it was not so with God from the beginning, it was not so with God then, now, or in the future. God is the same yesterday, today, and tomorrow. As we just read from Romans 1:28, *"God gave them over to a reprobate mind, to do those things which are not convenient."* Divorce from the time of Moses was rebellion against God's plan of marriage. *"24God also gave them up to uncleanness through the lusts of their own hearts, to dishonour their own bodies between themselves: 25Who changed the truth of God into a lie,"* states Romans 1:24-25. Changing the truth of God to fit our personal desires is changing the truth of God into a lie. Do not follow your own desires, follow God's desires! Proverbs 3:5-6 states, *"5Trust in the Lord with all thine heart; and lean not unto thine own understanding. 6In all thy ways acknowledge him, and he shall direct thy paths."*

Know this truth: In Matthew 19, Jesus was affirming the covenant of marriage, as God established it in Genesis 2:24: *"Therefore shall a man leave his father and his mother, and shall cleave unto his wife: and they shall be one flesh."* And we know with absolute certainty that Jesus was affirming this life-long covenant because He said so Himself in Matthew 19:4-6, when He responded to the Pharisees who tempted Him on interpreting the law. Jesus said, *"4Have ye not read, that he which made them at the beginning made them male and female, 5 And said, For this cause shall a man leave father and mother, and shall cleave to his wife: and they twain shall be one flesh? 6 Wherefore they are no more twain, but one flesh. What therefore God hath joined together, let not man put asunder."* This is Jesus stating and re-affirming Holy Scripture. The covenant of marriage is not to be broken

---

[17] Matthew 19:8.

by any man! One man, one woman, united together with God. This is the covenant of Marriage. Know this truth!

Furthermore, I have heard the argument, *"Divorce is allowable if either the husband or wife is unsaved."* This is not Scriptural! Those who argue such cite 2 Corinthians 6:14: *"Be ye not unequally yoked together with unbelievers: for what fellowship hath righteousness with unrighteousness? and what communion hath light with darkness?"*

However, they again take Holy Scripture out of context. They link the casual associations of believers with the covenant of marriage. This is error. This is changing the truth of God to fit our personal desires. This is changing, as Romans 1:25 states, *"the truth of God into a lie."* The Word of God speaks directly to this situation of a marriage involving a believer and a non-believer. In 1 Corinthians 7:10-14, we read of this and God's *"command"* to married couples:

> [10] And unto the married I command, yet not I, but the Lord, Let not the wife depart from her husband:

> [11] But and if she depart, let her remain unmarried or be reconciled to her husband: and let not the husband put away his wife.

> [12] But to the rest speak I, not the Lord: If any brother hath a wife that believeth not, and she be pleased to dwell with him, let him not put her away.

> [13] And the woman which hath an husband that believeth not, and if he be pleased to dwell with her, let her not leave him.

14 For the unbelieving husband is sanctified by the wife, and the unbelieving wife is sanctified by the husband: else were your children unclean; but now are they holy.

Marriages are established by God. And make no mistake, if it pleases God, it can be for the evangelization of the spouse, and this would be to the glory of God. Think about it! This is a powerful testament! *"The unbelieving husband is sanctified by the [believing] wife, and the unbelieving wife is sanctified by the [believing] husband."*[18] And as a result of this union, God assures us, *"else were your children unclean; but now are they holy."*[19] This is a blessing from God for those who abide by His Word.

Remember, you were called by God for the purpose of *"giving a blessing,"*[20] so *"that you might inherit a blessing."*[21] This applies to you, and if you are married, it applies to your relationship with your spouse. Honor this covenant, the sacred oath you took to God and your spouse, and believe in the power of God! Know it, use it, and share it! You will be a blessing to your spouse, to others, and your nation. 2 Chronicles 7:14 assures of this promise of God, *"If my people, which are called by my name, shall humble themselves, and pray, and seek my face, and turn from their wicked ways; then will I hear from heaven, and will forgive their sin, and will heal their land."* Count on it!

---

[18] 1 Corinthians 7:14.
[19] Ibid.
[20] 1 Peter 3:9.
[21] Ibid.

It is a simple principle of Scripture: Obey God and leave all the consequences to Him. I never heard this truth so simply stated, until I heard it from a godly man.[22] It was one of his life learning principles, gleamed from his 80-plus years of life, and a walk with God just shy of that. Yet, it is difficult for men, even impossible, to obey God. It is a matter of Faith that we obey, and, as Romans 10:17 states, *"So then faith cometh by hearing, and hearing by the Word of God."* Faith comes from God, and He speaks to us primarily through His Word, and through godly counsel from other believers based on Scripture, and through our circumstances. And this makes all the more sense when we examine the words of Jesus, when He spoke about faith in Matthew 19:26, *"With men this is impossible; but with God all things are possible."*

However, we are literally bombarded on the television and radio airwaves on the *"reasonableness"* of divorce. They say *"scars"* have been created that *"destroyed the marriage."* Know this: *"Scars"* are nothing but another word for *"strongholds,"* and they are not of God. Do not take refuge behind them! The Word of God commands us to dwell on good things, which are the things of God. And unfortunately, we hear from the profiteers of divorce at an ever increasing rate. And their campaigns against the institution of marriage are effective. They are the Pharisees of our time, and many just happen to be lawyers. To those who practice the evil arts contrary to the Word of God, I say, *"Woe unto you!"*

It deserves noting that I am an attorney and counselor at law, but a follower of Christ first. So I can comment on the legal profession in a manner much like the apostle Paul did on the disposition of the Jews at his revelation that he himself

---

[22] Dr. Charles F. Stanley, Senior Pastor, First Baptist Church of Atlanta.

was a Christian and one schooled in the Mosaic Law, as he was also a Pharisee.

The truth is: We have in our legal systems in America and around the world a stark clash with the Word of God. I will explain what I mean, and I will do so from a position of knowledge and experience. In addition to being an attorney and counselor at Law, and a former county judge, city chief judge, and a prosecutor, I was a professor of law at an American law school. I am quite familiar with the Law. But more importantly, I am familiar with the Word of God, and dedicated to a daily walk with the Lord, which includes reading and meditating on Holy Scripture each and every day. I hold fast to the proposition that Psalm 119:105 is true: *"Thy Word is a lamp unto my feet, and a light unto my path."*

In Mark 10:2-12, we read the following:

> 2 And the Pharisees came to him, and asked him, Is it lawful for a man to put away his wife? tempting him.
>
> 3 And he answered and said unto them, What did Moses command you?
>
> 4 And they said, Moses suffered to write a bill of divorcement, and to put her away.
>
> 5 And Jesus answered and said unto them, For the hardness of your heart he wrote you this precept.
>
> 6 But from the beginning of the creation God made them male and female.
>
> 7 For this cause shall a man leave his father and mother, and cleave to his wife;

8 And they twain shall be one flesh: so
then they are no more twain, but one
flesh.

9 What therefore God hath joined together,
let not man put asunder.

10 And in the house his disciples asked
him again of the same matter.

11 And he saith unto them, Whosoever
shall put away his wife, and marry
another, committeth adultery against her.

12 And if a woman shall put away her
husband, and be married to another, she
committeth adultery. [Mark 10:2-12]

God's admonishment is clear: *"What therefore God hath joined together, let not man put asunder."*[23] No man is allowed to break this Covenant, not the husband, not the wife, not the lawyer, and not the judge. *"Let not man,"*[24] is a clear admonition that no man is to interfere with or attempt to break this covenant of God!

The Bible repeatedly addresses how the hardness of hearts turns men [and women] from the Word of God. As Romans 1:28 notes, *"God gave them over to a reprobate mind, to do those things which are not convenient."* Divorce from the time of Moses was rebellion against God's plan of marriage. The same is true today! As Roman 1:24-25 observes, *"24God also gave them up to uncleanness through the lusts of their own hearts, to dishonour their own bodies between themselves: 25Who changed the truth of God into a lie."* Changing the truth of God to fit our personal desires, no matter who tells you it is alright to do so,

---

23 Mark 10:9.
24 Ibid.

be it a lawyer or judge, is changing the truth of God into a lie. Do not follow your own desires, follow God's desires! And listen to no man or woman who suggests a course of action that is in violation of Holy Scripture. Proverbs 3:5-6 states, *"5Trust in the Lord with all thine heart; and lean not unto thine own understanding. 6In all thy ways acknowledge him, and he shall direct thy paths."*

Yet, despite this truth, we see more than half of all marriages end in divorce, even amongst self-professed *"Christians."* And we are hard-pressed not to see billboard signs on any major highway promoting divorce by some lawyer. In fact, those kinds of advertisements are just about everywhere: on television, radio, the internet, you name it! Even in my home state of Georgia, we have something called *"no fault divorce."* It reminds me of *"no fault insurance."* We have so trivialized the sacred covenant of marriage that to end it is easier and often less expensive than coach airfare from one city to another. And, by the way, divorce is often promoted as a *"Special,"* meaning you can get one cheaper during limited *"sale"* times. It is disgusting and, most concerning, contrary to the Word of God!

And it is not only the so-called *"family law" and Divorce* lawyers promoting divorces who are at fault. It is the judges who casually grant divorce orders, and the legislatures who have enacted so-called *"no fault divorce"* laws that are to blame as well. This is no doubt *"heresy"* to most in today's legal profession, and I cannot help but think how tall the legal profession once stood many decades ago. That was a time when lawyers in America could be disbarred for advertising. And it was a time many lawyers understood and professed that our modern civil and criminal codes were based on the laws of God. How far, or perhaps how low, we have gone since those golden days! Lest I digress.

Hollywood and the world have trivialized divorce, even encouraged it, as has the modern legal profession. And even in present day America, we find individual states have by judicial fiat redefined *"Marriage"* from being between one man and one woman, to same-sex couples. And, like it did with the killing of babies in their mothers wombs, the Supreme Court has made same-sex *"Marriage"* the *"Law of the Land,"* essentially creating *"constitutional rights"* out of thin air, NOT the express words of the Constitution, which actually is the Law of the Land. Un-elected activist federal judges have redefined the meaning of marriage and its standing under the law, despite how *"We the people"* voted on such matters, or what the Word of God would suggest.

No doubt about it, Marriage is under attack, not only in the political arena, but in the spiritual realm as well. Satan is alive and well! Even the National Cathedral in our nation's capital, which is arguably the most prominent of America's churches, having hosted presidents and mourned national tragedies, has opted to perform marriage ceremonies for gay, lesbian, bisexual, and transgender members.

Like it or not, the Word of God says in Leviticus 18:22, *"Thou shalt not lie with mankind, as with womankind: it is abomination."* This is the express Word of God. Believe it or not. The church would do well to believe! But even such belief in the Word of God is under siege, with Liberal politicians calling such affirmations of the Christian faith *"hate speech,"* subject to criminal prosecution under Caesar's Law. We see these New Age laws enacted in Europe and Liberal bastions like California and New York.

But the real questions are: *What do I believe? And what should I do if I am having issues in my marriage?* The answers are: *Believe God! Seek God's answers through His Word. Seek godly counsel from believers, who can give godly advice. Seek out a pastor or a priest, knowledgeable and trusting in the Word of God.* Don't give up! And do not give into temptation! If you have to, contact me or believers you can find at the Lighthouse! This is the time to apply the admonition in 2 Corinthians 6:14: *"Be ye not unequally yoked together with unbelievers: for what fellowship hath righteousness with unrighteousness? and what communion hath light with darkness?"* Do not seek ungodly counsel! **My strong recommendation is not to seek advice from a divorce attorney.** I have personally witnessed these practitioners of evil, delighting themselves in encouraging, facilitating and advocating this darkness.

If you are a believer who had a divorce, or an abortion, you are not under condemnation. God loves you, unconditionally, and His mercy is great. If you are an attorney promoting divorce, woe unto you! And fellow-believers, if you know of someone contemplating divorce, share the Truth of God's Word. Be a blessing!

The ultimate truth is that without God, there is no anchor in Truth. It is the road that leads to destruction. So the only way to a godly life is through God. With Him, we have all of our needs met, marriages endure and grow, and we have an immovable, unchanging foundation when all about us retreat and fall. And God has promised to never leave or forsake us.[25] This is blessed assurance! A great Hope! *"Now faith is the substance of things hoped for,"* we read in Hebrews 11:1, *"the evidence of things not seen."* And as my dear friend,

---

[25] Hebrews 13:5.

Vickie Hafer,[26] shared with me in my greatest valley experience, *"Hope in the promises of God is the foundation of our Faith ... always Hope!"* How right she was ... and is! Proverbs 13:12 says, *"Hope deferred maketh the heart sick: but when the desire cometh, it is a tree of life."* So Hope! *"Be of good courage,"* says the psalmist in Psalm 31:24, *"and he shall strengthen your heart, all ye that hope in the Lord."* Hope[27] is essential to building the Faith!

Trust and obey God, and leave all the consequences to Him! You will be blessed for it! And you will be a blessing to others!

~~~~~~~~~

"What therefore God hath joined together, let not man put asunder."

~ Mark 10:9

---

[26] Vickie Hafer, Vice President & Ministries Director, Air Minister, The Lighthouse WECC 89.3 FM, St. Marys, GA.

[27] Psalm 16:9; Psalm 22:9; Psalm 21:3; Psalm 31:24; Psalm 33:18; Psalm 33:22; Psalm 38:15; Psalm 39:7; Psalm 42:5; Psalm 42:11; Psalm 43:5; Psalm 71:5; Psalm 71:14; Psalm 78:7; Psalm 119:43; Psalm 119:49; Psalm 119:74; Psalm 119:81; Psalm 119:114; Psalm 119:116; Psalm 119:147; Psalm 119:166; Psalm 130:5; Psalm 130:7; Psalm 131:3; Psalm 146:5; Psalm 147:11; Proverbs 10:28; Proverbs 13:12; Proverbs 14:32; Proverbs 19:18; Ecclesiastes 9:4; Jeremiah 14:8; Jeremiah 17:7; Jeremiah 17:13; Jeremiah 17:17; Jeremiah 31:17; Jeremiah 50:7; Lamentations 3:18; Lamentations 3:21; Lamentations 3:24; Lamentations 3:26; Lamentations 3:29; Ezekiel 13:6; Hosea 2:15; Joel 3:16; Zechariah 9:12; Acts 2:26; Acts 23:6; Acts 24:15; Acts 26:6; Acts 26:7; Romans 4:18; Romans 5:2; Romans 5:4; Romans 5:5; Romans 8:20; Romans 8:24; Romans 8:25; Romans 12:12; Romans 15:4; Romans 15:13; 1 Corinthians 9:10; 1 Corinthians 13:7; 1 Corinthians 13:13; 1 Corinthians 15:19; 2 Corinthians 3:12; 2 Corinthians 10:15; Galatians 5:5; Ephesians 1:18; Ephesians 4:4; Philippians 1:20; Colossians 1:5; Colossians 1:23; Colossians 1:27; 1 Thessalonians 1:13; 1 Thessalonians 2:19; 1 Thessalonians 5:8; 2 Thessalonians 2:16; 1 Timothy 1:1; Titus 1:2; Titus 2:13; Titus 3:7; Hebrews 3:6; Hebrews 6:11; Hebrews 6:18; Hebrews 6:19; Hebrews 7:19; Hebrews 11:1; 1 Peter 1:3; 1 Peter 1:13; 1 Peter 1:21; 1 Peter 3:15; 1 John 3:3.

Chapter 3

All Things are Possible with God

"But Jesus beheld them, and said unto them, With men this is impossible; but with God all things are possible."

~Matthew 19:26

"This book of the law shall not depart out of thy mouth; but thou shalt meditate therein day and night, that thou mayest observe to do according to all that is written therein: for then thou shalt make thy way prosperous, and then thou shalt have good success."

~ Joshua 1:8

"And Jesus looking upon them saith, With men it is impossible, but not with God: for with God all things are possible."

~ Mark 10:27

It is not enough to read the words of this book. They must be understood and applied. This is Faith in action! In James 2:17, we read, *"Even so faith, if it hath not works, is dead, being alone."* Faith is a motivator to do good works, but it must be in concert with the Spirit. This synergy allows us to do what the world deems *"impossible."*

For example, if we were burdened financially, having marital problems, health problems, or trouble with friendships, our tendency would be to preoccupy our time worrying or being anxious. But what does the Word of God say we should do?

In the Book of Philippians, we read:

> [6] Be anxious for nothing, but in everything by prayer and supplication with thanksgiving let your requests be made known to God.
>
> [7] And the peace of God, which surpasses all comprehension, will guard your hearts and your minds in Christ Jesus. [Philippians 4:6-7, NASB]

The power and simplicity of this passage is awesome!

First, we are commanded to *"Be anxious for nothing,"*[28] meaning, we are not to be troubled by the challenges of the day. Remember, 2 Timothy 1:7 tells us, *"For God hath not given us the spirit of fear; but of power, and of love, and of a sound mind."* Being anxious or having fear in our walk is not of God. Anxiousness and fear do nothing to resolve problems or improve your health or promote positive relationships. In fact, they hinder us in our walk, and they do nothing positive. On the other hand, being poised and calm of spirit helps us focus and be in tune with our surroundings and our situation. It clears the mind and the heart, and prepares us to properly deal with whatever the troubling matter is.

Secondly, we are to pray to God.[29] This involves speaking directly to God. Yes, the Creator of the universe wants to hear from you! Proverbs 15:8 gives us insight to how

---

[28] Philippians 4:6, NASB.
[29] Philippians 4:6.

the Lord regards this truth, when it states, *"the prayer of the upright is His delight."* And Scripture tells us in 1 Peter 3:12, *"For the eyes of the Lord are over the righteous, and his ears are open unto their prayers."*

Thirdly, we are to make our petition directly to God. Ask Him. Scripture calls this *"supplication."*[30] And in Matthew 21:22, we read, *"And all things, whatsoever ye shall ask in prayer, believing, ye shall receive."* Make your request known to God. As James 4:2 states, *"...ye have not, because ye ask not."* Ask Him!

Finally, we are to thank God, because we know He loves us unconditionally, He is faithful, and He has promised not to forsake[31] us. We are commanded to give thanks in all things. In 1 Thessalonians 5:18 we read, *"In every thing give thanks: for this is the will of God in Christ Jesus concerning you."*

But the real question is: *Will this approach work?* Specifically, will it work for you? The answer is: *Yes!*

Perhaps the most powerful demonstration of this truth is found in the Gospel of John, Chapter 11. Here, Jesus is informed that a friend whom He loved, Lazarus, is sick.[32] And although Lazarus was far off, Jesus was not anxious. In fact, Scripture tells us He tarried where He was for two additional days.[33] This was perplexing to both His disciples and other friends of Lazarus, as they had seen Jesus heal the

---

[30] Philippians 4:6.

[31] Hebrews 13:5; Deuteronomy 4:31, 31:6, 31:8; 1 Chronicles 28:20; Psalm 94:14; Isaiah 41:17.

[32] John 11:3. *"Therefore his sisters sent unto him, saying, Lord, behold, he whom thou lovest is sick."*

[33] John 11:6. *"When he had heard therefore that he was sick, he abode two days still in the same place where he was."*

sick, and they wanted the same for Lazarus.[34]

Note, Jesus was not anxious at the news His friend was sick. He remained where He was for two additional days before journeying to the home of Lazarus. And Jesus actually knew Lazarus was dead.[35]

When He arrived at the home of Lazarus, Jesus proceeded to the gravesite of His friend. Jesus prayed to the Father,[36] having made His supplication for Lazarus to rise again,[37] and gave thanks to God.[38]

It is important to highlight here that this was all done before Lazarus was raised from the dead. It was only after (1) not being anxious, (2) praying, (3) making supplication, and (4) giving thanks to God, that Lazarus was raised from the dead.[39]

In this example, Jesus again sets the standard for walking in faith, and it is here He teaches us how to deal with troubles, regardless of their magnitude. Just as He instructed the disciples on how to pray,[40] Jesus was teaching His followers to live life to its fullest, with faith and power. With God, all things are possible![41]

---

[34] John 11:37. *"And some of them said, Could not this man, which opened the eyes of the blind, have caused that even this man should not have died?"*

[35] John 11:14. *"Then said Jesus unto them plainly, Lazarus is dead."*

[36] John 11:41. *"Then they took away the stone from the place where the dead was laid. And Jesus lifted up his eyes, and said, Father, I thank thee that thou hast heard me."*

[37] John 11:23. *"Jesus saith unto her, Thy brother shall rise again."*

[38] John 11:41. *"Then they took away the stone from the place where the dead was laid. And Jesus lifted up his eyes, and said, Father, I thank thee that thou hast heard me."*

[39] John 11:43-44. *"And when he thus had spoken, he cried with a loud voice, Lazarus, come forth. And he that was dead came forth, bound hand and foot with graveclothes: and his face was bound about with a napkin. Jesus saith unto them, Loose him, and let him go."*

[40] Matthew 6:9-13.

[41] Philippians 4:13. *"I can do all things through Christ which strengtheneth me."*

We are walking in faith and alive in Christ when the Spirit of God leads us to perform good works in our daily walk. As James notes, *"For as the body without the spirit is dead, so faith without works is dead also."*[42] Put your faith into action!

If we are in His will, He hears us, and He helps us. And if the answer to our prayerful request is not on our timetable, trust that He answers prayers perfectly. Yes, perfectly! He answers prayer at exactly the right time, and we know His remedy for anything that confronts us is infinitely better than any choice we would have made for ourselves on the matter. Now that is awesome!

~~~~~~~~~~

*"For if any be a hearer of the word, and not a
doer, he is like unto a man beholding his
natural face in a glass:
For he beholdeth himself, and goeth his way,
and straightway forgetteth
what manner of man he was."*

~ James 1:23-24

---

[42] James 2:26.

Chapter 4

Keep Your Tongue from Evil & Do Good

"To sum up, all of you be harmonious,
sympathetic, brotherly, kindhearted, and humble in spirit;
Not returning evil for evil or insult for insult, but giving a blessing instead;
For you were called for the very purpose that you might inherit a blessing.
For, The one who desires life, to love and see good days,
Must keep his tongue from evil and do good;
He must seek peace and pursue it.
For the eyes of the Lord are toward the righteous,
And His ears attend to their prayer,
But the face of the Lord is against those who do evil."

~ 1 Peter 3:8-12, NASB

I am always amazed at the simple and direct instructions contained in Holy Scripture for leading a godly life. Think about the above quote from 1 Peter 3:9, *"Not returning evil for evil or insult for insult, but giving a blessing instead; For you were called for the very purpose that you might inherit a blessing."* This totally diffuses bad feelings or potential arguments among people, not to mention family members or spouses. What an amazing concept that we should be *"a blessing"* to those we might encounter in our lives!

This is the simplicity and the power of the Holy Bible. It has all we need to understand and achieve a godly life, the keys to personal growth, and the path to success. It is God's gift to the human race, and contains the blueprint for successful living, how to help guide the ones we love, and to correct them when they are stumbling, and how to keep them on a successful path. As 2 Timothy 3:16-17 states, *"16All scripture is given by inspiration of God, and is profitable for doctrine, for reproof, for correction, for instruction in righteousness: 17That the man of God may be perfect, thoroughly furnished unto all good works."*

Having Faith in God is living life at its very best. It is living life with great and sometimes unimaginable success. It is doing the impossible! And Holy Scripture tells us that this success is not for a season, but a lifetime! It is true prosperity! Read and marvel at the words of Psalm 1:

> 1 Blessed is the man that walketh not in the counsel of the ungodly, nor standeth in the way of sinners, nor sitteth in the seat of the scornful.
>
> 2 But his delight is in the law of the LORD; and in his law doth he meditate day and night.
>
> 3 And he shall be like a tree planted by the rivers of water, that bringeth forth his fruit in his season; his leaf also shall not wither; and whatsoever he doeth shall prosper.
>
> 4 The ungodly are not so: but are like the chaff which the wind driveth away.
>
> 5 Therefore the ungodly shall not stand in the judgment, nor sinners in the congregation of the righteous.
>
> 6 For the LORD knoweth the way of the righteous: but the way of the ungodly shall perish.

Psalm 1 is a clear and common sense approach to life. This is godly living! To walk with other good and godly people, to avoid evil and scornful people, to follow the laws of God, to be a blessing to others, and know that godly living is the way to success and prosperity. These are the words and promises of God. Meditate on them and follow them!

With this in mind, let's take a look at the fundamentals of this all important Word of God. Is It Really Important? Who Wrote It? Does It apply to me?

Is the Holy Bible Really Important?

So the real first question we must answer is: *Is the Holy Bible really important?* The answer is: *Absolutely!* This must be distinctly understood, or nothing good can come from this wonderful journey I am about to relate. The Bible is the Word of God. It is His unfolding revelation to mankind. It is the key to immediate, short-term, long-term, and eternal prosperity and success.

In the Holy Bible, we read the following in John 1:1-5:

> [1] In the beginning was the Word, and the Word was with God, and the Word was God.
>
> [2] The same was in the beginning with God.
>
> [3] All things were made by Him; and without Him was not any thing made that was made.
>
> [4] In Him was life; and the life was the light of men.

5 And the light shineth in darkness; and
the darkness comprehended it not.

Through these verses, we find that the Word of God is key to walking in the light of God. Without It, we are walking in darkness.

And John 1:14, goes on to state, *"And the Word was made flesh, and dwelt among us, (and we beheld His glory, the glory as of the only begotten of the Father,) full of grace and truth."* This is Christ Jesus.

And know that speaking the Word of God is important because of its impact, as we shall see throughout this book. It actually changes lives! And you are instrumental in this process when you share the Gospel. Psalm 37:23 tells us, *"The steps of a good man are ordered by the LORD: and he delighteth in his way."* And as we read the Word of God and speak it to others, God tells us in Isaiah 55:11: *"So shall my word be that goeth forth out of my mouth: it shall not return unto me void, but it shall accomplish that which I please, and it shall prosper in the thing whereto I sent it."* Speaking the Word of God is powerful, and always serves God's purpose. So speak it!

Who Wrote the Holy Bible?

The Holy Bible was written by the hands of many godly men, starting with the writing of Genesis by Moses and ending with the Book of Revelation by the apostle John, who were inspired by the Holy Spirit. It was written over the span of 1400 years and covers more than 4000 years of mankind's history.

Sceptics will question how men could have written of events prior to their births *(such as by Moses in Genesis)* and following their deaths *(such as by the prophets and the apostle John in Revelation)*. But the mere fact that men accurately wrote of these events gives us insight into the Bible's true authorship. God revealed those things that we might otherwise not have known. In 2 Peter 1:21, we read: *"For the prophecy came not in old time by the will of man: but holy men of God spake as they were moved by the Holy Ghost."* The author of the Holy Bible is God, with the words penned by prophets and the holy men of old.

Does the Holy Bible Apply to Me?

Knowing that the Holy Bible is both important and an inspired work of God, it merits asking: *Does the Holy Bible apply to me?* The answer is an unequivocal: *Yes!*

If you desire to live a godly life, to grow personally, be successful, be righteous, and be a man or woman after God's own heart, then the Holy Bible is indispensable! As we noted earlier, and as 2 Timothy 3:16-17 states, *"16All scripture is given by inspiration of God, and is profitable for doctrine, for reproof, for correction, for instruction in righteousness: 17That the man of God may be perfect, thoroughly furnished unto all good works."* Know with all of your heart, and soul, and mind, it was written for you! You are special to God. Yes, the God who created the universe and made all things is personally interested in you and your future. Here is what God says: *"For I know the plans that I have for you,' declares the Lord, 'plans for welfare and not for calamity to give you a future and a hope."*[43] He gave you and me the Word so that we might have a restored close and personal

---

[43] Jeremiah 29:11, NASB.

relationship with Him. He loves you! Believe in Him, and trust Him! His Word applies to you!

But knowing these things and all that you read in this book will matter little if you do not take that leap of faith I spoke about earlier. This is a time of decision-making, that is, making a decision to believe in the power of God to change your life, or to pursue other paths. It is the choice we read about in the Book of Joshua. *"Now therefore fear the LORD, and serve him in sincerity and in truth: and put away the gods which your fathers served on the other side of the flood, and in Egypt; and serve ye the LORD,"* we read in Joshua 24:15, and the pivotal decision in the very next verse, *"And if it seem evil unto you to serve the LORD, choose you this day whom ye will serve; whether the gods which your fathers served that were on the other side of the flood, or the gods of the Amorites, in whose land ye dwell: but as for me and my house, we will serve the LORD."*[44] This is the choice: To follow the One True God or the gods of this world. Anything you place before Almighty God in your life is an idol, a god of this world. Living a godly life, with all the blessings it entails, is pretty simple, but you cannot do it on your own. It requires knowing and following God. As Jesus observed, *"With men this is impossible; but with God all things are possible."* So you make the decision!

Walking in Faith is synonymous with reading the Holy Bible and following God's plan for your life. And what is His plan for your life? It is: That you might read, meditate on, and apply Holy Scripture in your life. That you might walk in light, and not in darkness. That you might believe in His Son as your Lord and Saviour, and walk in the way of truth, success, and everlasting life!

---

[44] Joshua 24:16.

~~~~~~~~~~

*"Whether therefore ye eat, or drink, or whatsoever ye do,
do all to the glory of God."*

~ Psalm 37:23

Chapter 5

Know These Truths

God Loves You

"For God so loved the world, that he gave his only begotten Son,
that whosoever believeth in him should not perish, but have everlasting life."

~ John 3:16

God Knows You Better Than You Know Yourself

"But the very hairs of your head are all numbered.
Fear ye not therefore, ye are of more value than many sparrows."

~ Matthew 10:30-31

"Before I formed thee in the belly I knew thee;
and before thou camest forth out of the womb I sanctified thee,
and I ordained thee a prophet unto the nations."

~ Jeremiah 1:5

"'For I know the plans that I have for you,' declares the Lord,
'plans for welfare and not for calamity to give you a future and a hope.'"

~ Jeremiah 29:11, NASB

God Cares About You

"Casting all your care upon him; for he careth for you."

~ 1 Peter 5:7

"But my God shall supply all your need according
to his riches in glory by Christ Jesus."

~ Philippians 4:19

"I will not leave you comfortless: I will come to you."

~ John 14:18

Perhaps because of my military training, or more likely my insight from the Holy Spirit, I have learned that developing and keeping priorities are essential to success in whatever endeavor we are engaged. This is particularly true in a marriage and a family!

With this in mind, I have learned, and taught others, that keeping our focus on God is essential. Focusing on God builds Faith! While people and things of this world may fail us, God never does. He is our priority. In all things, we must first and foremost focus on God. We do this most effectively when we know these three things: (1) God loves you, (2) He knows you better than you know yourself, and (3) He cares about you! Let us discuss these three things and explain their importance in our lives, especially as we confront challenges on this journey of faith.

(1) **God Loves You!** This is the foundation of our faith, and something we need to know first and foremost. More personally, it is important to understand that God loves You! He made you in His image, with a specific plan and purpose for your life. All throughout Scripture we read about God's unconditional love for His children. One familiar passage so succinctly describes this love, but we often

fail to grasp the depth of its meaning. It is the most well-known verse in the Bible:

> For God so loved the world, that he gave his only begotten Son, that whosoever believeth in him should not perish, but have everlasting life. [John 3:16]

Faith in God is the fountain of all of life's blessings, and we must accept it to live life at its very best. And this love is eternal, as God, the author of love, tells us in Hebrews 13:5, *"I will never leave thee, nor forsake thee."* Jesus tells us in John 14:16-17, *"16And I will pray the Father, and he shall give you another Comforter, that he may abide with you for ever; 17Even the Spirit of truth; whom the world cannot receive, because it seeth him not, neither knoweth him: but ye know him; for he dwelleth with you, and shall be in you."* And if that is not reassuring enough, our Lord goes on in John 14:23 to state, *"If a man love me, he will keep my words: and my Father will love him, and we will come unto him, and make our abode with him."* God promises that He, the Father, Son, and Holy Spirit, will be in us. He loves us that much! He will never leave or forsake us! Know that God always keeps His promises,[45] as He is absolutely faithful.[46]

(2) **God Knows You Better than You Know Yourself!** As much as we think we know ourselves, God knows us infinitely better. He knew you and me before the foundations of the world,[47] He knows the number of hairs on our head,[48] and He knows our future. Without a doubt, He knows us better than we know ourselves!

---

[45] Hebrews 10:23, "...for He is faithful that promised."
[46] Deuteronomy 7:9; Psalm 36:5; Isaiah 49:7; 1 John 1:9.
[47] Ephesians 1:4.
[48] Matthew 10:30.

God's intimate knowledge of us is a testament to His love for us! The God who brought the very universe into existence[49] also knows the number of hairs on our heads.[50] And He tells us in Jeremiah 1:5, *"Before I formed thee in the belly I knew thee."* Cast out any doubt, God knows you better than you know yourself.

(3) **God Cares About You!** This is the great promise we can rest all of our hopes on! Jesus tells us in John 14:18 that because He cares about us, *"I will not leave you comfortless: I will come to you."* This is especially comforting in times of crisis. God cares so much about us that He declares in Isaiah 41:10:

> Fear not, for I *am* with you; Be not dismayed, for I *am* your God. I will strengthen you, Yes, I will help you, I will uphold you with My righteous right hand.

And we are further reassured in Philippians 4:19, when we read, *"...God will supply all your need according to His riches and glory by Christ Jesus."* We can take heart that this is an inexhaustible fulfilment of needs. There is no greater supplier of our needs. Trust Him!

Jeremiah 29:11 puts it all in perspective, *"'For I know the plans that I have for you,' declares the Lord, 'plans for welfare and not for calamity to give you a future and a hope.'"*

And remember this: Jesus said He came so that we, those who believe in Him as Saviour, might have life, and have it

---

[49] Genesis 1:1.
[50] Matthew 10:30.

more abundantly. As Jesus testified in John 10:10, *"I am come that they might have life, and that they might have it more abundantly."* This is the overflowing goodness and mercy of God. And in Psalm 34:7 God's Word further declares, *"Delight thyself also in the Lord: and he shall give thee the desires of thine heart."* As His children, He promises to care for us and meet all of our needs, and if we would do so little a thing as *"delight"* ourselves in Him, He will also give us the desires of our heart. How great is this mighty assurance?

No matter what befalls you, know this: God is on your side! He loves you, He knows you better than you know yourself, and He cares about you! With this knowledge and understanding, you are in good hands! In fact, you are in the best possible hands. His Word says, in 1 Peter 5:7, *"Casting all your care upon Him; for He careth for you."* With Him, your future is assured,[51] all your needs are met,[52] and all things are possible![53] You can take this journey of faith with trust and confidence in Him. Be of good cheer!

~~~~~~~~~~

"Thy word is a lamp unto my feet, and a light unto my path."

~ *Psalm 119:105*

---

[51] Jeremiah 29:11.
[52] Philippians 4:19.
[53] Matthew 19:26.

Chapter 6

YOU are Called for a Purpose

"'For I know the plans that I have for you,' declares the Lord,
'plans for welfare and not for calamity to give you a future and a hope.'"

~ Jeremiah 29:11, NASB

"And we know that all things work together for good to them that love God,
to them who are the called according to his purpose."

~ Romans 8:28

"Trust in the LORD with all thine heart;
and lean not unto thine own understanding.
In all thy ways acknowledge him, and he shall direct thy paths."

~ Proverbs 3:5-6

If you are human, the simple fact is that you have gone through some difficult times. They are a fact of life. No person in the history of man has gone through life without trials. Even Jesus had difficult times. But the real test is what happens when difficult times befall us. Do we reflect and ask, *"Why me?"* Do we dwell on negative things in an anxious state? After all, we are only human, right?

Interestingly enough, Jesus boldly addressed times of crisis and trials in one of His parables. In Luke 6:48-49, Jesus speaks of a flood that overtakes a neighborhood. The point is that every one of us experiences trials and heartaches in our lives. We are all confronted by potentially devastating situations. No one is immune from disasters like floods, loss of possessions, deaths in our families, divorce, feelings of inadequacy or loneliness, and the list goes on and on. But the meaning of this parable is that some are different. In this story, there was a man who dug deep into the ground and built the foundation of his house upon a rock, while the other merely built his home upon the soft earth. When the flood arose, the stream it created could not shake the home which was carefully built upon a solid foundation, but the other home suffered great ruin.

In this parable, we have two men, two humans, but one of them possesses wisdom and a power that compels him to better prepare and weather the storm and the flood that comes to all of us in this earthly life. As Psalm 34:19 states, *"Many are the afflictions of the righteous: but the LORD delivereth him out of them all."* I understand from personal experience that this is sometimes difficult to grasp, especially in times of intense personal trial. But always remember what God says, *"My grace is sufficient for thee: for my strength is made perfect in weakness."*[54] And it is in this revelation that the apostle Paul notes, *"Most gladly therefore will I rather glory in my infirmities, that the power of Christ may rest upon me."*[55] Know in your heart that through the trials of life, when we as believers in Christ are at our weakest, God is made strongest in us, and His power will never fail us! This is when we can move *"mountains."* He is absolutely faithful!

And, if I may, might I suggest you are infinitely more than just human? After all, if you are a believer in the Lord Jesus Christ, are you not indwelled by the Father, Son, and

---

[54] 2 Corinthians 12:9.
[55] 2 Corinthians 12:10.

Holy Spirit? Are you not safe on the solid foundation of the rock which is God? And is not the Holy Spirit with you to comfort, teach, and guide you in this walk of faith?

In John 14:23, *"Jesus answered and said unto him, If a man love me, he will keep my words: and my Father will love him, and we will come unto him, and make our abode with him."* This proves that the Father and the Son live in us. And Jesus went on in John 14:26, *"But the Comforter, which is the Holy Ghost, whom the Father will send in my name, he shall teach you all things, and bring all things to your remembrance, whatsoever I have said unto you."* These are the promises of God. Know them. Dwell on them. And take comfort and strength from them.

You can do all things through God! Philippians 4:13 says, *"I can do all things through Christ which strengtheneth me."* And this is true! But I would like to challenge you to apply it in your life. The Christian does this by declaring, *"I will do all things through Christ who strengthens me!"* This includes moving *"mountains!"*

When troubles befall you, turn to God. Ask Him, *"Lord, what are you teaching me through this matter?"* Grow closer to God through your trials. James 4:8 tells us, *"Draw nigh to God, and he will draw nigh to you."* Apply Holy Scripture, like Romans 8:28, which states, *"And we know that all things work together for good to them that love God, to them who are the called according to his purpose."* Note that Scripture says, *"All things work together for good,"* not just the pleasant things that come our way. Like it or not, we often learn the most valuable lessons when we stumble or face trial.

And as a cautionary note, do not waiver in your Faith! James tells us in James 1:5-8:

⁵If any of you lack wisdom, let him ask of God, that giveth to all men liberally, and upbraideth not; and it shall be given him.

⁶ But let him ask in faith, nothing wavering. For he that wavereth is like a wave of the sea driven with the wind and tossed.

⁷ For let not that man think that he shall receive any thing of the Lord.

⁸ A double minded man is unstable in all his ways.

So, be strong in your Faith! Do not waiver in your trust of God or His promises! Follow God's teachings and commands! And as I mention often in this book, always remember to give thanks to God. No matter what the situation, remember, He has allowed the matter to be brought to your attention for a good purpose. 1 Thessalonians 5:18 commands us, *"In every thing give thanks: for this is the will of God in Christ Jesus concerning you."* Do it! Trust that God is doing a great work in your life. You will be blessed!

Discovering God's plans for your life is important. God knows them, and it does not matter how old you are. In Jeremiah 29:11, we read, *"For I know the plans that I have for you,' declares the Lord, 'plans for welfare and not for calamity to give you a future and a hope."* You should know His plans as well. After all, it is like setting out on an important trip and not knowing your directions or destination. I would certainly hope we would give at least as much attention to God's plans for us as we would to our next planned vacation destination. It only makes sense.

So now we come to the question of the ages: *"What do we do to discover God's direction and plan for our lives?"* This is a great question, because it is like finding ourselves lost in the wilderness at night, with no idea of where we are or where to go. It can be a frightening predicament.

We first need to rely on an authority to solve this problem. Being lost in the forest, for example, we might rely on GPS or a compass and a map. But in navigating life, that is, discovering where we are and where we should go, well, that requires something special. The consequences are too great to leave this to mere chance. And I can think of no better authority or example to follow than that of the Lord Jesus Christ. Jesus was known by those closest to Him as a man of prayer,[56] a man who sought the Father, and read Scripture and applied It, especially when it came to defeating the temptations of the devil.[57] Jesus was intimately familiar with Scripture, even the prophesies that foretold of His coming, from His virgin birth in Bethlehem to His death on the cross, to His resurrection on the third day to His ultimate return. Jesus studied and applied Holy Scripture in His life as a human being. He did it, and you can too!

Reading, meditating on, and applying Holy Scripture is key to unlocking God's plans, and promises, and purpose for your life. You may ask, *"How can one Book, which has been read by billions of people, speak directly to me and my unique circumstances?"* It's a good question, and my answer is, the Bible is like a beautiful, captivating piece of fine art. It says something different and wonderful to each and every viewer studying its content. But the Bible is much more than that. It is the most important book ever written, or ever will be

---

[56] Luke 6:12.
[57] Luke 4:2-13.

written. It is the complete Word of God, what my pastor once called, *"the unfolding revelation"*[58] of God. You can read a passage of Holy Scripture more than once, and each time you read It you can discover new insight to Its powerful, timeless message. Passages often leap out at me, even after reading them before, because they are applicable to all situations and stages of life. Know in your heart that all of God's Word applies directly to you! The Bible is the key to discovering God's plans and promises and purpose for your life. Psalm 119:105 states it splendidly, *"Thy Word is a lamp unto my feet, and a light unto my path."* Study it! Use it! Illuminate your walk of Faith!

~~~~~~~~~~

"But Jesus beheld them, and said unto them, With men this is impossible; but with God all things are possible."

~Matthew 19:26

---

[58] Dr. Charles F. Stanley, Senior Pastor, First Baptist Church of Atlanta, 2012.

Chapter 7

The Power of Prayer

"Pray without ceasing."

~ 1 Thessalonians 5:17

*"Ye lust, and have not: ye kill, and desire to have, and cannot obtain:
ye fight and war, yet ye have not, because ye ask not."*

~ James 4:2

*"But without faith it is impossible to please him: for he that cometh to God must
believe that he is, and that he is a rewarder of them that diligently seek him."*

~ Hebrews 11:6

*"And the prayer of faith shall save the sick, and the Lord shall raise him up;
and if he have committed sins, they shall be forgiven him.
Confess your faults one to another, and pray one for another,
that ye may be healed.
The effectual fervent prayer of a righteous man availeth much."*

~ James 5:15-16

*"Call unto me, and I will answer thee,
and show thee great and mighty things, which thou knowest not."*

~ Jeremiah 33:3

"And all things, whatsoever ye shall ask in prayer, believing, ye shall receive."

~Matthew 21:22

Prayer is powerful! It is life changing and history making! The Holy Bible is replete with example after example on how God moves mightily in response to prayer. In my own life, I can attest to the power of prayer. Time after time after time, God hears our prayers and answers them in an awesome way, never failing to hear our pleas, and truly giving us more than we hoped for or deserved. These may be prayers for us or intercessory prayers on behalf of loved ones. God hears them all! This is the power of prayer!

God answers prayer even when we fall short in our own walk of faith. One shining example of this is a story in the Bible you might recall from childhood. It is the story of Samson, who was blessed by the Lord.[59] Samson was born during a time the Philistines had dominion over Israel.[60] It was God's plan for Samson that he would *begin to deliver Israel out of the hand of the Philistines.*"[61] And it was at this time the Lord God moved mightily in the life of Samson, so much so that when the Philistines moved to capture him, Judges 15:15 states, *"And he found a new jawbone of an ass, and put forth his hand, and took it, and slew a thousand men therewith."* Samson found favour with the Lord.

But Samson strayed from the safety and strength of God's will in his life when he took up with the Philistines, slept with a harlot, and engaged in an adulterous relationship with a conspirator who sought to betray him for a payment of silver. And betray him she did, as we read in Judges 16:6-21:

> 6 And Delilah said to Samson, Tell me, I
> pray thee, wherein thy great strength

---

[59] Judges 13:24.
[60] Judges 14:4.
[61] Judges 13:5.

lieth, and wherewith thou mightest be bound to afflict thee.

7 And Samson said unto her, If they bind me with seven green withs that were never dried, then shall I be weak, and be as another man.

8 Then the lords of the Philistines brought up to her seven green withs which had not been dried, and she bound him with them.

9 Now there were men lying in wait, abiding with her in the chamber. And she said unto him, The Philistines be upon thee, Samson. And he brake the withs, as a thread of tow is broken when it toucheth the fire. So his strength was not known.

10 And Delilah said unto Samson, Behold, thou hast mocked me, and told me lies: now tell me, I pray thee, wherewith thou mightest be bound.

11 And he said unto her, If they bind me fast with new ropes that never were occupied, then shall I be weak, and be as another man.

12 Delilah therefore took new ropes, and bound him therewith, and said unto him, The Philistines be upon thee, Samson. And there were liers in wait abiding in the chamber. And he brake them from off his arms like a thread.

[13] And Delilah said unto Samson, Hitherto thou hast mocked me, and told me lies: tell me wherewith thou mightest be bound. And he said unto her, If thou weavest the seven locks of my head with the web.

[14] And she fastened it with the pin, and said unto him, The Philistines be upon thee, Samson. And he awaked out of his sleep, and went away with the pin of the beam, and with the web.

[15] And she said unto him, How canst thou say, I love thee, when thine heart is not with me? thou hast mocked me these three times, and hast not told me wherein thy great strength lieth.

[16] And it came to pass, when she pressed him daily with her words, and urged him, so that his soul was vexed unto death;

[17] That he told her all his heart, and said unto her, There hath not come a razor upon mine head; for I have been a Nazarite unto God from my mother's womb: if I be shaven, then my strength will go from me, and I shall become weak, and be like any other man.

[18] And when Delilah saw that he had told her all his heart, she sent and called for the lords of the Philistines, saying, Come up this once, for he hath shewed me all his heart. Then the lords of the Philistines came up unto her, and brought money in their hand.

19 And she made him sleep upon her knees; and she called for a man, and she caused him to shave off the seven locks of his head; and she began to afflict him, and his strength went from him.

20 And she said, The Philistines be upon thee, Samson. And he awoke out of his sleep, and said, I will go out as at other times before, and shake myself. And he wist not that the LORD was departed from him.

21 But the Philistines took him, and put out his eyes, and brought him down to Gaza, and bound him with fetters of brass; and he did grind in the prison house.

And although Samson strayed from God's commandments, and paid dearly for his transgressions, God still loved him. In fact, God would answer Samson's prayer even in the final moments of his mortal life, as we read in the next and final verses of Judges 16:

22 Howbeit the hair of his head began to grow again after he was shaven.

23 Then the lords of the Philistines gathered them together for to offer a great sacrifice unto Dagon their god, and to rejoice: for they said, Our god hath delivered Samson our enemy into our hand.

24 And when the people saw him, they praised their god: for they said, Our god hath delivered into our hands our enemy, and the destroyer of our country, which slew many of us.

25 And it came to pass, when their hearts were merry, that they said, Call for Samson, that he may make us sport. And they called for Samson out of the prison house; and he made them sport: and they set him between the pillars.

26 And Samson said unto the lad that held him by the hand, Suffer me that I may feel the pillars whereupon the house standeth, that I may lean upon them.

27 Now the house was full of men and women; and all the lords of the Philistines were there; and there were upon the roof about three thousand men and women, that beheld while Samson made sport.

28 And Samson called unto the LORD, and said, O Lord God, remember me, I pray thee, and strengthen me, I pray thee, only this once, O God, that I may be at once avenged of the Philistines for my two eyes.

29 And Samson took hold of the two middle pillars upon which the house stood, and on which it was borne up, of the one with his right hand, and of the other with his left.

30 And Samson said, Let me die with the Philistines. And he bowed himself with all his might; and the house fell upon the lords, and upon all the people that were therein. So the dead which he slew at his death were more than they which he slew in his life.

31 Then his brethren and all the house of his father came down, and took him, and brought him up, and buried him between Zorah and Eshtaol in the buryingplace of Manoah his father. And he judged Israel twenty years. [Judges 16:22-31]

In his final acts as a man, Samson prayed to God, sought His strength, and destroyed all the lords of the Philistines. This is the power of prayer. On that day, Samson returned to the purpose and plan God had for his life to begin freeing His chosen people from oppression, and killed more of the enemies of the Lord than he had in his entire life. Samson, despite his frailties, loved God. And what was meant for evil by the Philistines was turned into good by God, proving the great truth of Romans 8:28: *"And we know that all things work together for good to them that love God, to them who are the called according to his purpose."*

Prayer opens the door to indescribable peace, understanding, and power. Prayer is our means of direct communication with the Creator of the universe. So pray!

Perhaps one of the most powerful illustrations on the power capable of being unleashed by prayer was found in an encounter in the Garden of Gethsemane. As Jesus was about to be taken by the servants of the high priests and the elders, Peter struck one of the servants of the high priest with a sword. Matthew 26:52-54 records the Lord's response:

> 52 Then said Jesus unto him, Put up again thy sword into his place: for all they that take the sword shall perish with the sword.
>
> 53 Thinkest thou that I cannot now pray to my Father, and he shall presently give me more than twelve legions of angels?
>
> 54 But how then shall the scriptures be fulfilled, that thus it must be?

In these few simple verses, Jesus revealed His destiny was the fulfilment of God's will, that is, to be both God and man and live and die as a substitute for you and me in our sin judgment. And as easy as it would have been for Jesus to avoid His suffering and stop His crucifixion and atonement for our sins, He loved us so much that He suffered the penalty for our transgressions, so that our sins might be forgiven and our relationship with God might be restored, and we might have everlasting life with Him.

Note, Jesus said He could *"now pray to my Father, and he shall presently give me more than twelve legions of angels."* This was a powerful declaration on the ability of prayer to manifest the awesome power of God in our lives. And it was a sobering testament to our Lord's strict adherence to doing the will of God.

The Old Testament is replete with vivid depictions of the awesome, destructive power of angels. In Genesis 19, God sent just two angels to destroy the city of Sodom,[62] and destroy it they did.[63] In 2 Kings 19, when the battle-hardened

---

[62] Genesis 19:13.
[63] Genesis 19: 24-25.

Assyrian army, led by their king, Sennacherib, surrounded Jerusalem and threatened to utterly destroy God's chosen people, Holy Scripture notes the King of Judah prayed to the Lord.[64] Verse 19 records the words of Hezekiah, King of Judah, *"Now therefore, O LORD our God, I beseech thee, save thou us out of his hand, that all the kingdoms of the earth may know that thou art the LORD God, even thou only."* God answered that prayer and sent a single angel that night, which killed 185,000 Assyrians. 2 Kings 19:35 records the carnage, *"And it came to pass that night, that the angel of the LORD went out, and smote in the camp of the Assyrians an hundred fourscore and five thousand: and when they arose early in the morning, behold, they were all dead corpses."*

It suffices knowing that if one angel could lay waste to 185,000 Assyrian soldiers on one given night, just imagine what the *"twelve legions of angels"* that Jesus spoke of could have done. Understand a single legion of angels would be the numerical equivalent of a Roman legion of 3,000 to 6,000 soldiers. That would make the force Jesus spoke of anywhere between 36,000 to 72,000 angels. Such a force the world has never known. It could lay waste to the entire planet, even today. These are testaments to the power of prayer and the compassion and love of God.

A knowledge and understanding of prayer would be incomplete without knowing what Jesus Himself said about the subject. In Matthew 6:5-18, Christ Jesus shares with us how to pray and where to pray, and He speaks on the subject of fasting as well:

> [5] And when thou prayest, thou shalt not be as the hypocrites are: for they love to

---

[64] 2 Kings 19:15.

pray standing in the synagogues and in the corners of the streets, that they may be seen of men. Verily I say unto you, They have their reward.

6 But thou, when thou prayest, enter into thy closet, and when thou hast shut thy door, pray to thy Father which is in secret; and thy Father which seeth in secret shall reward thee openly.

7 But when ye pray, use not vain repetitions, as the heathen do: for they think that they shall be heard for their much speaking.

8 Be not ye therefore like unto them: for your Father knoweth what things ye have need of, before ye ask him.

9 After this manner therefore pray ye: Our Father which art in heaven, Hallowed be thy name.

10 Thy kingdom come, Thy will be done in earth, as it is in heaven.

11 Give us this day our daily bread.

12 And forgive us our debts, as we forgive our debtors.

13 And lead us not into temptation, but deliver us from evil: For thine is the kingdom, and the power, and the glory, for ever. Amen.

14 For if ye forgive men their trespasses, your heavenly Father will also forgive you:

15 But if ye forgive not men their trespasses, neither will your Father forgive your trespasses.

16 Moreover when ye fast, be not, as the hypocrites, of a sad countenance: for they disfigure their faces, that they may appear unto men to fast. Verily I say unto you, They have their reward.

17 But thou, when thou fastest, anoint thine head, and wash thy face;

18 That thou appear not unto men to fast, but unto thy Father which is in secret: and thy Father, which seeth in secret, shall reward thee openly.

In these few but powerful passages, Jesus shares the purpose, nature, and power of prayer. First, prayer is a private, personal communication with Almighty God. It begins with an acknowledgement that He is Holy, and the Lord of our lives and of the entire universe. We are then instructed to make supplication, that is, to request His provision for our lives, which is a petition for all that we need to accomplish His goal for our lives. Next, we are instructed to seek forgiveness from God for any transgressions, to the same degree we forgive others who have offended us. This is not only a blessing to us, but a blessing to others. In this respect, we reap what we sow, knowing this is the will of our heavenly Father. And finally, Jesus instructs us to seek God's protection from the wiles of the devil, that is, to show us favour and lead us in a godly walk, keeping us from all things evil.

Toward the conclusion of the Lord's Prayer (Matthew 6:9-13), we note the importance of asking God to deliver us from evil. And by no coincidence, this was our Lord's earthly ministry: Jesus delivered the oppressed from evil. On one occasion, the apostles were ministering in the manner of Christ, but were unable to expel the devil from a child they encountered. Seeing this thing, Jesus rebuked the devil, and cast him out of the child;[65] when the apostles asked Him why they could not cast out the devil,[66] Jesus shared the power of prayer, combined with fasting, and declared in Matthew 17:21, *"Howbeit this kind goeth not out but by prayer and fasting."* This is why Jesus also instructs us in fasting in Matthew 6:16-18. Prayer and fasting are an essential part of our walk as Christians.

And in all things, including prayer and fasting, we are to give thanks to God for the great privilege of being His children, a part of His kingdom, and as such the recipients of His grace and His power and His glory. As *1 Thessalonians 5:18* states, *"In every thing give thanks: for this is the will of God in Christ Jesus concerning you."* So give God thanks!

Prayer is powerful. Godly men have known this throughout history. And the important thing to remember is that people may change, but God never changes. He is the same yesterday, today, and tomorrow. He is faithful, and longs for an intimate relationship with each and every one of us. This is why He sent His Son! He hears and answers our prayers. What an awesome blessing!

Dr. Jerry Falwell once told me something that Chrysostom, an early church father in the latter days of the Roman Empire, had said about the power of prayer. This

---

[65] Matthew 17:18.
[66] Matthew 17:19.

quote had *"great meaning"* to Dr. Falwell:[67]

> The potency of prayer hath subdued the strength of fire; it hath bridled the rage of lions, hushed anarchy to rest, extinguished wars, appeased the elements, expelled demons, burst the chains of death, expanded the gates of heaven, assuaged diseases, repelled frauds, rescued cities from destruction, stayed the sun in its course, and arrested the progress of the thunderbolt.
>
> *~~~John Chrysostom, 349-407 A.D., born in Antioch, and considered an important early church father. He ministered during the time of the Roman Emperor Theodosius I. Chrysostom was Archbishop of Constantinople, who served under Pope Innocent I, and was venerated as a saint soon after his death. The Orthodox and Eastern Catholic Churches honor him as a saint.*

How true! Prayer has done all these things and more! Such is the power of prayer! It is Faith in action! What was true about God yesterday is true today … and forever! God loves you, He hears you, and He answers prayer! So pray!

~~~~~~~~~~

"Call unto me, and I will answer thee,
and show thee great and mighty things, which thou knowest not."

~ Jeremiah 33:3

---

[67] Dr. Jerry Falwell, at Thomas Road Baptist Church, Lynchburg, Virginia, September 12, 1993.

Chapter 8

Foundations of the Faith

"In the beginning was the Word,
and the Word was with God, and the Word was God."

~ John 1:1

"Jesus Christ the same yesterday, and today, and forever."

~ Hebrews 13:8

"Thy word is a lamp unto my feet, and a light unto my path."

~ Psalm 119:105

"So then faith cometh by hearing, and hearing by the word of God."

~ Romans 10:17

"Enter ye in at the strait gate: for wide is the gate, and broad is the way,
that leadeth to destruction, and many there be which go in thereat:
Because strait is the gate, and narrow is the way, which leadeth unto life,
and few there be that find it."

~ Matthew 7:13-14

"For God so loved the world, that he gave his only begotten Son,
that whosoever believeth in him should not perish, but have everlasting life."

~ John 3:16

"For the preaching of the cross is to them that perish foolishness;
but unto us which are saved it is the power of God."

~ 1 Corinthians 1:18

"Then one of them, which was a lawyer, asked him a question, tempting him, and saying, Master, which is the great commandment in the law? Jesus said unto him, Thou shalt love the Lord thy God with all thy heart, and with all thy soul, and with all thy mind. This is the first and great commandment. And the second is like unto it, Thou shalt love thy neighbour as thyself. On these two commandments hang all the law and the prophets."

~ Matthew 22:35-40

"This book of the law shall not depart out of thy mouth; but thou shalt meditate therein day and night, that thou mayest observe to do according to all that is written therein: for then thou shalt make thy way prosperous, and then thou shalt have good success."

~ Joshua 1:8

"But my God shall supply all your need According to his riches in glory by Christ Jesus."

~ Philippians 4:19

"Let us hear the conclusion of the whole matter: Fear God, and keep his commandments: for this is the whole duty of man."

~ Ecclesiastes 12:13

Romans 1:17 says, *"For therein is the righteousness of God revealed from faith to faith: as it is written, The just shall live by faith."* These are powerful words!

Let's face it: We live in a corrupt world. The Word of God is cast aside for selfish desires and political correctness. We condone same-sex marriage, the murder of our unborn children, and when it comes down to it, many who call themselves *"believers"* prefer to follow their feelings and emotions rather than obey God's Word. \With this said, we should resolutely heed the admonition of God in Isaiah 5:20, *"Woe unto them that call evil good, and good evil; that put darkness for light, and light for darkness; that put bitter for sweet, and sweet for bitter!"*

The truth is: People change, but God does not! As my friend Vickie Hafer so often reminded me, *"God is not a man that He would change His mind."* How true! Now that is godly counsel! God is the same yesterday, today, and tomorrow.[68] And the beauty of the Holy Bible is that we can actually see God at work in it: His presence in the history of man, His nature and abilities, His unconditional love, His mercy, His grace, His omnipresence, His omnipotence, His will for our lives, His promises, and His commandments. God is real!

God is the foundation of our faith, our hope, our love, and our very existence. And He reveals the nature of this foundation for His children in Ephesians 2:19-22:

> [19] Now therefore ye are no more strangers and foreigners, but fellowcitizens with the saints, and of the household of God;
>
> [20] And are built upon the foundation of the apostles and prophets, Jesus Christ himself being the chief corner stone;
>
> [21] In whom all the building fitly framed together groweth unto an holy temple in the Lord:
>
> [22] In whom ye also are builded together for an habitation of God through the Spirit.

---

[68] Hebrews 13:8.

This is the foundation of our faith. We *are "of the household of God."*[69] And the Lord Jesus Christ is the *"chief corner stone"*[70] of this foundation. Thus, any good to come of this book is based on your relationship with God. It is not just an understanding, it is an acceptance of Jesus as Lord and our Saviour, and our surrender to His will. This is the key to personal growth and the way to a successful life.

I began this chapter, and every chapter of this book, with verses of Holy Scripture. They inspire. They edify. They lift the spirit! And as powerful as they are, they only scratch the surface of the world of wonder and enlightenment that awaits you in the Word of God! Seize this moment to dedicate a portion of each and every day to the study of Holy Scripture. Learn the ways of God and His plan for you and your success, and how you can achieve it. It is that simple! Do it!

I have heard it said, *"I barely have time to read the Bible once a week, let alone every day!"* To that, I respectfully say, *"Nonsense!"* If you do not have time to read the Word of God each and every day, then I suggest you are not wisely using your time. I cannot imagine starting each day without reading the Holy Bible, and seeing God's plan for my walk that day. And I would not feel at ease going to sleep each night without hearing the Word of God, and meditating on that Truth before and during my slumber. Psalm 119:105 states, *"Thy word is a lamp unto my feet, and a light unto my path."* I prefer to walk in His light. How about you?

If you believe that you can do without the Word of God in your daily walk, then I suggest you are too arrogant. If you

---

[69] Ephesians 2:19.
[70] Ephesians 2:20.

feel like you do not need to know the will of God, and you can do it alone, then you are too prideful. But whether you are too arrogant, prideful, or just plain foolish, you are a mere phone call away from disaster, and a heartbeat away from eternity. I humbly suggest you re-evaluate your walk.

The Word of God is the ultimate authority on the Kingdom of God and the foundation for a faith to fully realize the power of God in your life. Read it, and apply it to your life!

Repent! And seek the Kingdom of God!

~~~~~~~~~~

"This book of the law shall not depart out of thy mouth; but thou shalt meditate therein day and night, that thou mayest observe to do according to all that is written therein: for then thou shalt make thy way prosperous, and then thou shalt have good success."

~ Joshua 1:8

Chapter 9

The Greatest of These is Love

*"If I speak with the tongues of men and of angels, but do not have love,
I have become a noisy gong or a clanging cymbal. If I have the gift of prophecy,
and know all mysteries and all knowledge; and if I have all faith, so as to remove
mountains, but do not have love, I am nothing. And if I give all my possessions to
feed the poor, and if I surrender my body to be burned,
but do not have love, it profits me nothing.*

*Love is patient, love is kind and is not jealous; love does not brag and is not
arrogant, does not act unbecomingly; it does not seek its own, is not provoked,
does not take into account a wrong suffered, does not rejoice in unrighteousness,
but rejoices with the truth; bears all things, believes all things, hopes all things,
endures all things.*

*Love never fails; but if there are gifts of prophecy, they will be done away;
if there are tongues, they will cease; if there is knowledge, it will be done away.*

But now faith, hope, love, abide these three; but the greatest of these is love."

~ 1 Corinthians 13:1-8, 13, NASB

Love is a gift from God. It is the realization that the Creator of the universe genuinely cares about you and your welfare. His greatest priority for your life is for you to come to a personal relationship with Him.[71] It is the reason He created man, and it is the reason why He created you! It is the reason He sent His only begotten Son, even after man had sinned and turned his back on Him, so you and I could have a restored relationship with God the Father. It is the new and everlasting

---

[71] Stanley, C.F. (2008). *30 Life Principles*. Atlanta: In Touch Ministries.

covenant that creates an unbreakable, unshakeable bond with God.

In 1 John 4:16, we read *"God is love."* But let us explore the qualities of Love, which after all are the qualities of God. 1 Corinthians 13:4-8 [NASB] tells us, *"4 Love is **patient**, love is **kind** and is **not jealous**; love does **not brag** and is **not arrogant**, 5 does **not act unbecomingly**; it does **not seek its own**, is **not provoked**, does **not take into account a wrong suffered**, 6 does **not rejoice in unrighteousness**, but **rejoices with the truth**; 7 bears all things, believes all things, hopes all things, endures all things. 8 Love **never fails**."* Know these things, meditate on them, and live them! They are essential to your marriage!

Knowing these qualities is important for several reasons, but the primary reasons are (1) God gives us this insight into His nature in His Word, and (2) we are told by the apostle Paul, in Romans 8:29, *"to be conformed to the image of His Son."* This means God is sharing His qualities with us because it is important to Him that we know what being a disciple of His Son entails, or He would not have revealed this to us in His Word. It means living a life that is patient, kind, not jealous, without bragging or arrogance, nor acting unbecoming, it is thinking of others, not being provoked, and keeping no record of wrongs committed against you by loved ones, especially family members, or even your spouse; it means forgiveness. It means rejoicing in the things of God, and not those things that are evil. It means bearing all things, believing in all the promises of God, hoping all things, and enduring all things. It means understanding that God, who is Love, never fails! I say again: God never fails! Count on it! Love is indispensable, and the key to living a godly life!

Furthermore, 1 John 4:16-21 addresses the meaning of love and its presence in our lives. Commit yourself to understanding these precepts. They are important to God, and as such, should be important to us:

[16] And we have known and believed the love that God hath to us. God is love; and he that dwelleth in love dwelleth in God, and God in him.

[17] Herein is our love made perfect, that we may have boldness in the day of judgment: because as he is, so are we in this world.

[18] There is no fear in love; but perfect love casteth out fear: because fear hath torment.

[19] He that feareth is not made perfect in love.
We love him, because he first loved us.

[20] If a man say, I love God, and hateth his brother, he is a liar: for he that loveth not his brother whom he hath seen, how can he love God whom he hath not seen?

[21] And this commandment have we from him, That he who loveth God love his brother also.

This is a powerful testament, as it assures us that if we dwell in love, we dwell in God, and God dwells in us. It is a theme we read throughout the New Testament, that is, God abides in those who believe on His Son for their salvation. It is the great hope and promise of our faith. You need never fear when God abides in you.[72] He reassures use that *"perfect love casteth out fear,"* and points to the evidence of the strength of His love, especially when He states, *"he who loveth God love his brother also."* This is the depth and breadth and power of Love in our lives! Jesus loves us unconditionally, and we are to conform to His image and love our neighbors.

There is a difference when we have God in our lives. Man without God cannot love unconditionally. We hate at the slightest provocation. But God loves us unconditionally, no matter what we do. Man is limited. God is all powerful. Having God in our lives changes everything. This is why Jesus said in Matthew 19:26, *"With men this is impossible; but with God all things are possible."* This is the power of God in our lives!

And if you were wondering why God ranked Love above Faith and Hope,[73] think about it. God is love,[74] and existed before the foundations of the world,[75] and even past the end of this age.[76] Faith and hope, on the other hand, really won't exist in the end, because, as 1 John 3:2 declares, *"Beloved, now are we the sons of God, and it doth not yet appear what we shall be: but we know that, when He shall appear, we shall be like Him; for we shall see Him as He is."* All of our faith and hope will then be fulfilled, and we will dwell for an eternity in Love. This is the promise of God. Believe it!

~~~~~~~~~~

---

[72] John 14:16, 23.
[73] 1 Corinthians 13:13.
[74] 1 John 4:16.
[75] John 17:24.
[76] Matthew 28:20.

"But now faith, hope, love, abide these three;
but the greatest of these is love."

~ *1 Corinthians 13:13, NASB*

Chapter 10

The Fruit of the Spirit

"But the fruit of the Spirit is love, joy, peace, patience, kindness, goodness, faithfulness, gentleness, self-control; against such things there is no law."

~ Galatians 5:22-23, NASB

"So God created man in his own image, in the image of God created he him; male and female created he them. And God blessed them, and God said unto them, Be fruitful, and multiply, and replenish the earth, and subdue it: and have dominion over the fish of the sea, and over the fowl of the air, and over every living thing that moveth upon the earth."

~ Genesis 1:27-28

In my own walk of faith, I have on occasion heard people say, *"I'm not sure if I'm saved."* And these words are always spoken with a great deal of emotion. In fact, I have heard these words uttered by many people, including people who profess to know Christ. It is a question of uncertainty that deserves a wise answer, an answer based on what the Word of God says.

When a man or woman believes and accepts the fact that Jesus Christ is Lord and came in the flesh and lived among us, and died on the cross, as our substitutionary sacrificial intercessor,[77] and rose again[78] so our relationship with God

---

[77] 1 John 4:10: *"Herein is love, not that we loved God, but that he loved us, and sent his Son to be the propitiation for our sins."*

could be restored, we are *"saved"* and *"born again."* This saving event or *"salvation"* brings us into a personal relationship with the Lord, with the promise of God that the Holy Spirit will indwell us from that point in our walk, and we will have eternal life with God. As Romans 6:23 states, *"For the wages of sin is death; but the gift of God is eternal life through Jesus Christ our Lord."* And Scripture gives us evidence of this salvation in the life of a person:

> 16 Ye shall know them by their fruits. Do men gather grapes of thorns, or figs of thistles?
>
> 17 Even so every good tree bringeth forth good fruit; but a corrupt tree bringeth forth evil fruit.
>
> 18 A good tree cannot bring forth evil fruit, neither can a corrupt tree bring forth good fruit.
>
> 19 Every tree that bringeth not forth good fruit is hewn down, and cast into the fire.
>
> 20 Wherefore by their fruits ye shall know them. [Matthew 7:16-20]

This *"good fruit"* is from God, as He is the source of all that is *"good."*[79] Thus, *"good"* in man comes from God, and is manifested in the life of the Christian through the *"Fruit of the Spirit,"* which Galatians 5:22-23 defines as *"22love, joy, peace, patience, kindness, goodness, faithfulness, 23gentleness, [and] self-control."* Those who are saved have these fruits through the indwelling of the Holy Spirit. But it is important to

---

[78] Romans 10:9.
[79] Mark 10:18; Psalm 106:1; Psalm 118:1; Psalm 118:29; Psalm 119:68; Psalm 136:1; Proverbs 4:2.

understand that these fruit grow as we grow in our personal relationship with the Lord. Being impatient does not mean you are not saved. It may just mean that this fruit will develop as your walk in faith develops. Remember, you may possess more gentleness than patience, or vice versa. No two people are the same, but for Christians, the Spirit that dwells within us is the same.[80] And we complement one another as Christians in the body of Christ.[81] Each bearing good fruit as the Spirit moves to feed the body of believers all to the glory of God.

I find no option in Holy Scripture for followers of Christ not to be fruitful. All disciples of Christ are commanded to be fruitful, without exception. We are repeatedly commanded by Holy Scripture to be fruitful.[82] Jesus spoke with particular clarity on this in the city of Bethany, when He used a particular fig tree as a metaphor for the absence of spiritual fruit. *"And when he saw a fig tree in the way, he came to it, and found nothing thereon, but leaves only, and said unto it, Let no fruit grow on thee henceforward for ever,"* said the Lord in Matthew 21:19, *"And presently the fig tree withered away."* A fig tree is cultivated for its fruit, which is the edible fig. This is why they are grown. It is a blessing to the hungry. If a fig tree does not bear good fruit and serve the purpose of its existence, it is useless. As Luke 6:44 states, *"For every tree is known by his own fruit. For of thorns men do not gather figs, nor of a bramble bush gather they grapes."*

But there is a staunch warning for us in Matthew 7:17 about fruit, *"Even so every good tree bringeth forth good fruit; but a corrupt tree bringeth forth evil fruit."* The truth is : there is evil

---

[80] 1 Corinthians 12:4-13.
[81] 1 Corinthians 12:14-27.
[82] Genesis 1:28; Genesis 9:1.

fruit, and that fruit is not of God, but is the way of destruction. As Matthew 7:21-27 notes:

> [21] Not every one that saith unto me, Lord, Lord, shall enter into the kingdom of heaven; but he that doeth the will of my Father which is in heaven.

> [22] Many will say to me in that day, Lord, Lord, have we not prophesied in thy name? and in thy name have cast out devils? and in thy name done many wonderful works?

> [23] And then will I profess unto them, I never knew you: depart from me, ye that work iniquity.

> [24] Therefore whosoever heareth these sayings of mine, and doeth them, I will liken him unto a wise man, which built his house upon a rock:

> [25] And the rain descended, and the floods came, and the winds blew, and beat upon that house; and it fell not: for it was founded upon a rock.

> [26] And every one that heareth these sayings of mine, and doeth them not, shall be likened unto a foolish man, which built his house upon the sand:

> [27] And the rain descended, and the floods came, and the winds blew, and beat upon that house; and it fell: and great was the fall of it.

Evil fruit is a threat to the Christian, and as such the body of Christ. It seeks to spread false doctrine. Its goal is to keep us from knowing and doing the will of God, and fulfilling the purpose of our lives, as it fosters spiritual deception and accusation. It was prevalent in the early church and it is here today. This is why we need to walk about with the Whole Armour of God. Knowing Holy Scripture makes us discerning of the wiles of the devil.

We are taught in Holy Scripture to test the spirits to know whether they are of God. This is done by knowing the Word of God, and comparing what It says to that which we are told. There are many false doctrines, but only one true Word of God. If someone, no matter who that person is, tells us something contrary to the Word of God, we are not to believe them or do as they might ask on the matter. Knowing what God says is critical to our success. Only then can you walk with authority in the Word of God.

1 John 4:1-6 states the following about testing the spirits and knowing who we are in the plan of God:

> [1] Beloved, believe not every spirit, but try the spirits whether they are of God: because many false prophets are gone out into the world.

> [2] Hereby know ye the Spirit of God: Every spirit that confesseth that Jesus Christ is come in the flesh is of God:

> [3] And every spirit that confesseth not that Jesus Christ is come in the flesh is not of God: and this is that spirit of antichrist, whereof ye have heard that it should come; and even now already is it in the world.

⁴ Ye are of God, little children, and have overcome them: because greater is he that is in you, than he that is in the world.

⁵ They are of the world: therefore speak they of the world, and the world heareth them.

⁶ We are of God: he that knoweth God heareth us; he that is not of God heareth not us. Hereby know we the spirit of truth, and the spirit of error.

Always be on guard with what others tell you the Bible says. Read it for yourself! The Holy Spirit will guide you, and teach you on the things of God, and enable you to bear good fruit. You will discover Truth, discernment, and power. As Christ Jesus assures us in John 15:16, *"I have chosen you, and ordained you, that ye should go and bring forth fruit, and that your fruit should remain: that whatsoever ye shall ask of the Father in my name, he may give it you."*

~~~~~~~~~

"But the fruit of the Spirit is love, joy, peace, patience, kindness, goodness, faithfulness, gentleness, self-control; against such things there is no law."

~ Galatians 5:22-23, NASB

Chapter 11

Dwell on Good Things

"Finally, brethren, whatever is true, whatever is honorable, whatever is right, whatever is pure, whatever is lovely, whatever is of good repute, if there is any excellence and if anything worthy of praise, dwell on these things."

~~~ Philippians 4:8, NASB

In Psalm 143:10 we read, *"Teach me to do thy will; for thou art my God: thy spirit is good; lead me into the land of uprightness."* That is what the Word of God does: It teaches us about God's will for our lives. And it does not take long for every follower of Christ to see the will of God for him or her in Holy Scripture.

The opening verse of Holy Scripture for this chapter points the way for every Christian toward a positive and godly path. It tells us to *"dwell"* on *"honorable"* and *"right"* and *"pure"* and *"lovely"* things, not on dishonorable, wrong, dark, or hateful things. We are encouraged to lift that which is *"good"* and *"excellent,"* not to promote evil or praise foolishness. This is in keeping with our character as followers of Christ, always conforming to His image.

Understand, there are consequences to not dwelling on good things. And the primary consequences are (1) breaking fellowship with God, in that, while He still loves you unconditionally, you have chosen not to obey His command that we *"dwell on these things;"*[83] (2) developing anxiety, depression, guilt, and hostility, which causes us to deviate from the will of God and lose friendships and our sense of purpose; and (3) it opens the door to satan having a stronghold in our lives, which hinders our personal growth and blocks the path to a successful life.

Satan uses the strongholds he obtains in people. I have heard some people substitute the word *"scars"* for strongholds in their lives. I equate the word *"scars"* with *"strongholds"* because they are one and the same negative influences in our lives. Saying we have *"scars"* from a relationship is just another acknowledgement that an ungodly *"stronghold"* exists. Nowhere in Scripture does God encourage use to reflect upon *"scars"* or any negatives feelings about family members or acquaintances. To the contrary, God commands us to dwell on good things![84] Guilt is another one of his weapons. Never listen to, or follow the directions of, someone who says, *"If you love me, you will do this ...,"* especially if it is contrary to the Word of God. This is someone attempting to plant the seeds of guilt in your life, or exploit them if they are already there! Resist the wiles of the devil. Nothing that violates Holy Scripture is from God.

1 Peter 5:8 warns us that *"your adversary the devil, as a roaring lion, walketh about, seeking whom he may devour."* And in his arsenal of weapons, he uses lies, deceit, anxiety, and guilt. He tries to tell us that God doesn't love us, or we are not good enough for God's love. He wants us to dwell on things that are not of God. The devil would have us dwell on the wrong things.

---

[83] Philippians 4:8, NASB.
[84] Philippians 4:8.

We have all done things in our lives that we regret, wrong things, evil things, but God tells us to *"repent,"*[85] that is, change direction. Jesus assures us that we are *"new creatures"*[86] in and through Him. As it is written in 1 Corinthians 5:17, *"Therefore if any man be in Christ, he is a new creature: old things are passed away; behold, all things are become new."* Satan would have us believe we need to feel guilty, as if our sin debt was not paid in full by Christ Jesus at the cross. Satan's goal is to hinder us, and distract us from our God-given mission. Christ absolutely paid our sin debt in full! We are children of God, washed white as snow, meaning free from sin and guilt, by the atoning blood of His Son.[87]

Be on guard against the wiles of the devil. He would have us embrace guilt and walk in his ungodly will. Stay clear from it! Cling to God, and dwell on good things!

All too often, we hear the voices of our age promoting things that are not honorable, or right, or pure, or lovely. It is these voices which praise the vilest of figures in our society. They champion lewd and violent behavior in their songs and conduct. They are the workers of iniquity. *"[22]Professing themselves to be wise, they became fools,"* states Romans 1:22-23, *"[23]And changed the glory of the uncorruptible God into an image made like to corruptible man, and to birds, and to fourfooted beasts, and creeping things."*

And the most alarming part of being among these voices of our age is their future. Note what Romans 1:24-32 says of them:

---

[85] Matthew 4:17; Matthew 9:13; Mark 1:15; Mark 2:17; Luke 5:32; Luke 13:3, 5; Luke 17:3, 4; Revelation 2:5, 16; Revelation 3:3, 19.

[86] 1 Corinthians 5:17.

[87] Matthew 26:28; Mark 14:24; Luke 22:20.

24 Wherefore God also gave them up to uncleanness through the lusts of their own hearts, to dishonour their own bodies between themselves:

25 Who changed the truth of God into a lie, and worshipped and served the creature more than the Creator, who is blessed for ever. Amen.

26 For this cause God gave them up unto vile affections: for even their women did change the natural use into that which is against nature:

27 And likewise also the men, leaving the natural use of the woman, burned in their lust one toward another; men with men working that which is unseemly, and receiving in themselves that recompence of their error which was meet.

28 And even as they did not like to retain God in their knowledge, God gave them over to a reprobate mind, to do those things which are not convenient;

29 Being filled with all unrighteousness, fornication, wickedness, covetousness, maliciousness; full of envy, murder, debate, deceit, malignity; whisperers,

30 Backbiters, haters of God, despiteful, proud, boasters, inventors of evil things, disobedient to parents,

31 Without understanding, covenantbreakers, without natural affection, implacable, unmerciful:

[32] Who knowing the judgment of God, that they which commit such things are worthy of death, not only do the same, but have pleasure in them that do them.

It is a sad future, but remember that with God all things are possible.[88] God has given us the answer to all negativity: His Son! Jesus died a substitutionary death for our sins -- past, present and future -- so that we might have life, and have it more abundantly. We are to repent, that is, turn away from dwelling on the wrong things and turn to dwelling on good, and trust He will handle the rest. Take your concerns to God! This is achieving peace of mind with God and living life at its very best!

~~~~~~~~~~

"Trust in the LORD with all thine heart;
and lean not unto thine own understanding.
In all thy ways acknowledge him, and he shall direct thy paths."

~ Proverbs 3:5-6

---

[88] Matthew 19:26.

Chapter 12

The Whole Armour of God

"Finally, my brethren, be strong in the Lord, and in the power of his might.
Put on the whole armour of God,
that ye may be able to stand against the wiles of the devil.
For we wrestle not against flesh and blood, but against principalities,
against powers, against the rulers of the darkness of this world,
against spiritual wickedness in high places.
Wherefore take unto you the whole armour of God,
that ye may be able to withstand in the evil day, and having done all, to stand.
Stand therefore, having your loins girt about with truth,
and having on the breastplate of righteousness;
And your feet shod with the preparation of the gospel of peace;
Above all, taking the shield of faith, wherewith ye shall be able to quench all the
fiery darts of the wicked.
And take the helmet of salvation, and the sword of the Spirit,
which is the word of God:
Praying always with all prayer and supplication in the Spirit,
and watching thereunto with all perseverance and supplication for all saints;
And for me, that utterance may be given unto me,
that I may open my mouth boldly,
to make known the mystery of the gospel,
For which I am an ambassador in bonds:
that therein I may speak boldly, as I ought to speak."

~ Ephesians 6:10-20

I have heard life called a *"struggle."* One acquaintance went so far as to call it being in a state of *"war!"* He described it as, *"a seemingly endless series of crises, occasionally interrupted by boredom."* And this was from the mouth of a successful man by worldly standards. He had money, notoriety, a big home, and an expensive car, but he was missing something in his life. Can you guess what it is?

If you have been reading this book thus far and haven't figured out he was missing the presence of God in his life, then I have done a poor job of presenting the Good News of the Gospel and the power of God in our lives. Of course, he was missing that which gives our life meaning, purpose, direction, and hope: the Lord Jesus Christ. And that, my friends, is a sad existence. It is not only a sad earthly existence, but an eternal death sentence. There is just no easy way to put this: Without the Lord Jesus Christ, you are separated from God and doomed to an eternity in hell. This is the sad truth of it all! But as you may have gathered through your reading, I prefer to dwell on good things … about you and, if you are fortunate enough, your marriage!

2 Corinthians 4:8-12, describes a battle field:

> 8 We are troubled on every side, yet not distressed; we are perplexed, but not in despair;
>
> 9 Persecuted, but not forsaken; cast down, but not destroyed;
>
> 10 Always bearing about in the body the dying of the Lord Jesus, that the life also of Jesus might be made manifest in our body.
>
> 11 For we which live are always delivered unto death for Jesus' sake, that the life also of Jesus might be made manifest in our mortal flesh.
>
> 12 So then death worketh in us, but life in you.

The Christian has awesome assurances from God. *"Who shall separate us from the love of Christ?"* asks the apostle Paul in Romans 8:35, *"shall tribulation, or distress, or persecution, or famine, or nakedness, or peril, or sword?"*

Well, Paul goes on to answer that question in Romans 8:37, *"Nay, in all these things we are more than conquerors through him that loved us."* Think about that: *"We are more than conquerors through [Christ Jesus]."* This is the power of God!

And he shares the absolute bond of the Christian to the Lord Jesus Christ in the following two verses (Romans 8:38-39): *"38For I am persuaded, that neither death, nor life, nor angels, nor principalities, nor powers, nor things present, nor things to come, 39Nor height, nor depth, nor any other creature, shall be able to separate us from the love of God, which is in Christ Jesus our Lord."* Now that is blessed assurance!

But what about those who might rise against us in our walk of faith? What about those who might falsely accuse us? Or seek our destruction? What about those who might work evil against us?

By no coincidence, Holy Scripture has an answer to these questions as well: *"No weapon that is formed against thee shall prosper; and every tongue that shall rise against thee in judgment thou shalt condemn,"* declares Isaiah 54:17, *"This is the heritage of the servants of the LORD, and their righteousness is of me, saith the LORD."* Those who believe on the Lord dwell under His protection. Proverbs 30:5 notes, *"Every word of God is pure; He is a shield unto them that put their trust in Him."* This is but a glimpse into the love and protection of Almighty God in the lives of His followers.

And if that was not enough, Psalm 84:11 states, *"For the LORD God is a sun and shield: the LORD will give grace and glory: no good thing will he withhold from them that walk uprightly."* This is not only protection, but favour and direction from God. These are daily blessings!

This direction from God in walking uprightly is shared by the apostle Paul in his first epistle to the church in Thessalonica [1 Thessalonians 5:5-24]. In one of his earliest writings, around the years 51-52 A.D., practical instruction in living a godly life, and introduces fellow-Christians to the Armour of God,[89] namely the Helmet of Salvation[90] and the Breastplate of Righteousness.[91]

> [5] Ye are all the children of light, and the children of the day: we are not of the night, nor of darkness.
>
> [6] Therefore let us not sleep, as do others; but let us watch and be sober.
>
> [7] For they that sleep sleep in the night; and they that be drunken are drunken in the night.
>
> [8] But let us, who are of the day, be sober, putting on the breastplate of faith and love; and for an helmet, the hope of salvation.
>
> [9] For God hath not appointed us to wrath, but to obtain salvation by our Lord Jesus Christ,

---

[89] Ephesians 6:11.
[90] Ephesians 6:17.
[91] Ephesians 6:14.

10 Who died for us, that, whether we wake or sleep, we should live together with him.

11 Wherefore comfort yourselves together, and edify one another, even as also ye do.

12 And we beseech you, brethren, to know them which labour among you, and are over you in the Lord, and admonish you;

13 And to esteem them very highly in love for their work's sake. And be at peace among yourselves.

14 Now we exhort you, brethren, warn them that are unruly, comfort the feebleminded, support the weak, be patient toward all men.
15 See that none render evil for evil unto any man; but ever follow that which is good, both among yourselves, and to all men.

16 Rejoice evermore.

17 Pray without ceasing.

18 In every thing give thanks: for this is the will of God in Christ Jesus concerning you.

19 Quench not the Spirit.

20 Despise not prophesyings.

21 Prove all things; hold fast that which is good.

22 Abstain from all appearance of evil.

> 23 And the very God of peace sanctify you wholly; and I pray God your whole spirit and soul and body be preserved blameless unto the coming of our Lord Jesus Christ.
>
> 24 Faithful is he that calleth you, who also will do it. [1 Thessalonians 5:5-24]

Less than a decade later, in the years of our Lord 60-62 A.D., the apostle Paul reveals the Whole Armour of God in his epistle to the Asian churches, amongst which was the foremost of the Christian churches in Ephesus. The epistle informed new congregations of their spiritual blessings, and the favour God bestowed on all followers of His Son. It also describes the battlefield upon which the forces of good and evil dwell, and the armaments they possess. The Whole Armour of God, described by Paul in Ephesians 6:10-20, was provided so that we might stand against the wiles of the devil. And in this light, it is appropriate to consider the opposing battlefield leaders, namely God and the devil. \The devil is powerful, but he is not all powerful. He can only do what God allows him to do, and this is particularly noteworthy when it comes to Christians.[92] Only God is all powerful, or "omnipotent,"[93] as Holy Scripture states. And God is everywhere, as He is omnipresent. The devil is limited to where he can be and what he can do. Satan roams the earth;[94] therefore, he cannot be in more than one place at a time. God indwells every Christian,[95] at the same time, no matter where they are. And our Lord God is omniscient, in that He knows all things, with absolute understanding and awareness. Knowing Holy Scripture reveals these truths, and the means

---

[92] Psalm 29:11; Psalm 119:165.
[93] Revelation 19:6.
[94] Job 1:7
[95] Matthew 18:20; John 14:15-17, 23; Hebrews 13:5; 1 John 4:16.

by which we effectively avoid and combat evil and live a godly life. The truth is: Satan is a defeated foe!

Know God:
This Comes From Reading the Holy Bible

"Finally, my brethren, be strong in the Lord,
and in the power of his might.
Put on the whole armour of God,
that ye may be able to stand against the wiles of the devil."

~ Ephesians 6:10-11

Know the Enemies of God:
The Devil, the World, and the Flesh.

"For we wrestle not against flesh and blood,
but against principalities, against powers,
against the rulers of the darkness of this world,
against spiritual wickedness in high places."

~ Ephesians 6:12

Fight the Good Fight:
Obey God and Leave All the Consequences to Him

"Wherefore take unto you the whole armour of God,
that ye may be able to withstand in the evil day,
and having done all, to stand."

~ Ephesians 6:13

Know the Truth of God:
Father, Son, & Holy Spirit
(Salvation comes only through His Son, Christ Jesus)

"Stand therefore, having your loins girt about with truth, and having on the breastplate of righteousness;"

~ Ephesians 6:14

Walk in the Knowledge of the Gospel

"And your feet shod with the preparation of the gospel of peace;"

~ Ephesians 6:15

Live by Faith:
Believe God's Word is Absolute Truth

"Above all, taking the shield of faith, wherewith ye shall be able to quench all the fiery darts of the wicked."

~ Ephesians 6:16

Salvation Rests in Christ Alone & Knowing Holy Scripture
Counters Spiritual Deception & Accusations
(Jesus said this & taught this when encountered by satan in the wilderness)

"And take the helmet of salvation, and the sword of the Spirit, which is the word of God:"

~ Ephesians 6:17

Prayer is Powerful:
Pray for Yourself and Others,
making specific requests to be in the will of God

"Praying always with all prayer and supplication in the Spirit,
and watching thereunto with all perseverance
and supplication for all saints;"

~ Ephesians 6:18

"And for me, that utterance may be given unto me,
that I may open my mouth boldly,
to make known the mystery of the gospel,
For which I am an ambassador in bonds:
that therein I may speak boldly, as I ought to speak."

~ Ephesians 6:19-20

Therefore, my brothers and sisters in Christ, put on the Whole Armour of God!

~~~~~~~~~~

"Finally, my brethren, be strong in the Lord, and in the power of his might.
Put on the whole armour of God,
that ye may be able to stand against the wiles of the devil."

~ Ephesians 6:10-11

"Submit yourselves therefore to God.
Resist the devil, and he will flee from you."

~ James 4:7

Chapter 13

Making & Knowing Friends

*"A man that hath friends must shew himself friendly:
and there is a friend that sticketh closer than a brother."*

~ Proverbs 18:24

*"Henceforth I call you not servants;
for the servant knoweth not what his lord doeth:
but I have called you friends;
for all things that I have heard of my Father I have made known unto you."*

~ John 15:15

"Iron sharpeneth iron; so a man sharpeneth the countenance of his friend."

~ Proverbs 27:17

*"Finally, be ye all of one mind, having compassion one of another, love as
brethren, be pitiful, be courteous: Not rendering evil for evil, or railing for railing:
but contrariwise blessing; knowing that ye are thereunto called,
that ye should inherit a blessing."*

~ 1 Peter 3:8-9

Making friends is often a difficult thing to do in our daily walk. There is great evil in our world. But the truth of the matter is: if you want to make friends, then you need to be friendly.[96]

---

[96] Proverbs 18:24.

Time and again, we see simple and direct instructions contained in Holy Scripture for achieving success, whether it be making friends or building Faith. Friends smile and are welcoming. They dwell on good things about one another. They speak the truth and share intimate things. Friends do not return anger for anger. They understand not everyone has a great day every day. We are prone to having moods, both positive and negative, and being led by emotions. Grouchiness, for lack of a better word, happens, even amongst the best of friends. Holy Scripture says to show yourself *"friendly"*[97] if you want friends. It does not say, *"Be friendly only when others are friendly to you!"* We are to be *"friendly"*[98] even when others are unfriendly toward us. Friends develop bonds that transcend all other acquaintances.

Friends have duties to one another. They think the best of one another, and they desire good for one another. They follow the example of Christ. When times are tough, friends share burdens and pray for one another. It is during times like these that friends notice the facial expressions and feelings of those whom they have befriended. Holy Scripture calls this observing the *"countenance"*[99] of a friend. And it is something observed by God. We read about His first such observation in the Book of Genesis in regard to Cain,[100] and thereafter observations of countenance are mentioned repeatedly

---

[97] Proverbs 18:24.

[98] Ibid.

[99] Proverbs 27:17.

[100] Genesis 4:5-6: *"But unto Cain and to his offering he had not respect. And Cain was very wroth, and his countenance fell. And the Lord said unto Cain, Why art thou wroth? and why is thy countenance fallen?"*

throughout the Word of God.[101] We are bound by Holy Scripture to help sharpen and lift the countenance of friends. This is what is meant in Proverbs 27:17 when we read, *"Iron sharpeneth iron; so a man sharpeneth the countenance of his friend."* This is an act of edification we are called to do.

Of course, the way to lose a friend is to violate those bonds and duties. Not supporting your friendship, sharing confidences that were meant only for you as a friend, or by lying, or perhaps doing anything that would identify you as being unfriendly, would be cause for losing a friend. And, in that light, consider your character and reputation. Is what you do consistent with a follower of Christ? If you are known as someone who is unfriendly in word or deed, or your bad works, chances are you will not find friends worth having. It is always best to build upon your personal relationship with Christ, and conform to His image. You will never be alone!

Understand, people make mistakes, but the key to success is learning from them. And it is here we demonstrate the quality and virtue of mercy and forgiveness. Friends show mercy and forgiveness to friends. I have always found it more desirable to keep friends and learn from mistakes, preferably the mistakes of others, as opposed to making those mistakes myself. And in this regard, understand good friends forgive and show mercy, and bear the fruit of the Spirit, which includes *"love, joy, peace, patience, kindness, goodness, faithfulness, gentleness, [and] self-control"* [*Galatians 5:22-23, NASB*]. These are the outward signs that God dwells in us.

---

[101] Genesis 4:5-6; 1 Samuel 1:18; 1 Samuel 16:12; 1 Samuel 17:42; 1 Samuel 25:3; 2 Samuel 14:27; Songs 2:14; Daniel 1:15; Daniel 5:6, 9, 10; Daniel 7:28; Daniel 8:23; Proverbs 15:13, 23; Proverbs 27:17; 2 Kings 8:11; Ezekiel 27:35; Nehemiah 2:2, 3; Ecclesiastes 7:3; Job 14:20; Job 29:24; Psalm 4:6; Psalm 10:4; Psalm 41:11; Psalm 42:5; Psalm 43:5; Psalm 44:3; Psalm 80:16; Psalm 89:15; Psalm 90:8; Luke 9:29.

I have been blessed with a few great friends. Some I have known for a relatively short time in my life, others for decades, but all are blessings from God. I think of friends that transcend the bounds of time and distance, like Arnold Mount. Arnie is a Vietnam veteran and retired U.S. Navy officer. We first met during my first tour of service as a judge, then my second, and later as a colleague when I served as a university vice president. He has stuck by me like a brother, seeing past my faults, and dwelling on only the good. And friends like Kathe Loeffler, Jay Krause, Guerry Bowen, and Shannon Brock, all of whom have a special place in my life and growth as a better person. And then there are people like Paul and Vickie Hafer, godly people who I have leaned on in the darkest of times and deepest of valleys in my life. Always there! Like Christ! They have never let me down! It is my prayer that you have friends such as these. What a blessing!

But the awesome revelation of this chapter is not how to make friends or how many friends you may have. Rather, it is the knowledge that *"there is a friend that sticketh closer than a brother."*[102] This is an express reference in Holy Scripture to the Lord Jesus Christ. It is an absolute statement and promise to those who accept Jesus Christ as their Lord and Saviour, and follow His commands.

As Christ Jesus states in John 15:15, *"Henceforth I call you not servants; for the servant knoweth not what his lord doeth: but I have called you friends; for all things that I have heard of my Father I have made known unto you."* The unfortunate truth of this verse is: Unsaved people know nothing of the friendship of Christ. God still loves them, but they are lost in their sin. They live a profoundly sad existence.

---

[102] Proverbs 18:24.

We who follow the Lord Jesus Christ are blessed beyond measure! We might err and fall short, perhaps even turn our back on God in our most trying times, but He has promised in Hebrews 13:5, *"I will never leave thee, nor forsake thee."* This is an absolute and unconditional friend. *"A friend,"* as Holy Scripture tells us, *"that sticketh closer than a brother."*[103] This is the central meaning of the new covenant,[104] not God visiting or walking with His people as was the case in the Old Testament,[105] but God abiding in His people, as we read in the New Testament.[106] This was the mission of Christ Jesus, that is, to restore our personal relationship with God. And that is why the veil that separated man from God was torn at that moment on the cross.[107] And He did that for you!

~~~~~~~~~~

"A man that hath friends must shew himself friendly:
and there is a friend that sticketh closer than a brother."

~ *Proverbs 18:24*

---

[103] Proverbs 18:24.
[104] Matthew 26:28, NKJV: *"For this is My blood of the new covenant, which is shed for many for the remission of sins."*; Matthew 26:28; Mark 14:24; Luke 22:20.
[105] Genesis 5:22, 24; Genesis 6:9; Psalm 55:14.
[106] Matthew 18:20; John 14:15-17, 23; Hebrews 13:5; 1 John 4:16.
[107] Matthew 27:50-54.

Chapter 14

The Gathering of the Saints

"Not forsaking the assembling of ourselves together, as the manner of some is;
but exhorting one another: and so much the more,
as ye see the day approaching."

~ Hebrews 10:25

"For as the body is one, and hath many members,
and all the members of that one body, being many, are one body:
so also is Christ. For by one Spirit are we all baptized into one body,
whether we be Jews or Gentiles, whether we be bond or free; and have been all
made to drink into one Spirit. For the body is not one member, but many.
If the foot shall say, Because I am not the hand, I am not of the body; is it therefore
not of the body? And if the ear shall say, Because I am not the eye, I am not of the
body; is it therefore not of the body? If the whole body were an eye, where were the
hearing? If the whole were hearing, where were the smelling?

But now hath God set the members every one of them in the body,
as it hath pleased him. And if they were all one member, where were the body?
But now are they many members, yet but one body. And the eye cannot say unto
the hand, I have no need of thee: nor again the head to the feet, I have no need of
you. Nay, much more those members of the body, which seem to be more feeble, are
necessary: And those members of the body, which we think to be less honourable,
upon these we bestow more abundant honour; and our uncomely parts have more
abundant comeliness. For our comely parts have no need: but God hath tempered
the body together, having given more abundant honour to that part which lacked.
That there should be no schism in the body; but that the members should have the
same care one for another. And whether one member suffer, all the members suffer
with it; or one member be honoured, all the members rejoice with it. Now ye are
the body of Christ, and members in particular. And God hath set some in the
church, first apostles, secondarily prophets, thirdly teachers, after that miracles,
then gifts of healings, helps, governments, diversities of tongues."

~ 1 Corinthians 12:12-28

We live in a fallen and dangerous world. This is a sad truth, and by all reports it appears things are not getting better. Even in America, where the torch of liberty is supposed to burn brightest, we see a rapid falling away from the founding principles. Our highest Court has removed prayer and the 10 Commandments from our public schools. They divined a *"right"* in our Constitution of a *"woman's privacy,"* which legally sanctions the abortion of more than a million babies a year in America, while at the same time hypocritically decrying the death of a infinitesimally smaller number of children by evil men in school shootings. Are babies in the womb of less value than babies in elementary school? I pray not. The killing of any child is horrific. Children are a gift from God. And we see the sanctioning of same-sex marriage, despite the fact it is also contrary to the Word of God. We see evil called *"good,"* and good called *"narrow-minded"* and *"evil."* Isaiah 5:20 warns, *"Woe unto them that call evil good, and good evil; that put darkness for light, and light for darkness; that put bitter for sweet, and sweet for bitter!"*

But as bad as things are, they could be worse. Whenever I ponder the state of affairs in America or around the world, I think back to the story of Sodom and Gomorrah in Genesis. Abraham was troubled by the knowledge that God's judgment was at hand for these cities, and asked, *"Wilt thou also destroy the righteous with the wicked?"*[108] And God considered Abraham's prayer and promised to spare His terrible, swift judgment from those cities if there could be

---

[108] Genesis 18:23.

found just ten righteous men there.[109] The sad truth is not even ten good men could be found. Those cities were so exceedingly wicked that God utterly destroyed them.[110]

It is my conviction God has kept His protective hand on America because righteous men and women can be found. Hopefully, you encounter these righteous men and women every day in your walk. However, if you do not, may I respectfully suggest you find them at the nearest Bible-believing church to your home?

Holy Scripture admonishes us *"not to forsake the assembling of ourselves together,"*[111] that is, fellow-believers whom He calls *"saints"*[112] and *"righteous"*[113] and *"holy,"*[114]

---

[109] Genesis 18:32.
[110] Genesis 19: 24-25.
[111] Hebrews 10:25.
[112] 1 Samuel 2:9; 2 Chronicles 6:41; Psalm 16:3; Psalm 30:4; Psalm 31:23; Psalm 34:9; Psalm 37:28; Psalm 50:5; Psalm 52:9; Psalm 85:8; Psalm 89:5, 7; Psalm 97:10; Psalm 116:15; Psalm 132:9, 16; Psalm 145:10; Psalm 148:14; Psalm 149:1, 5, 9; Daniel 7:18, 21, 22, 25, 27; Hosea 11:12; Zechariah 14:5; Matthew 27:52; Acts 9:13, 32, 41; Acts 26:10; Romans 1:7; Romans 8:27; Romans 12:13; Romans 15:25, 26, 31; Romans 16:2, 15; 1 Corinthians 1:2; I Corinthians 6:1, 2; 1 Corinthians 14:33; 1 Corinthians 16:1, 15; 2 Corinthians 1:1; 2 Corinthians 8:4; 2 Corinthians 9:1, 12; 2 Corinthians 13:13; Ephesians 1:1, 15, 18; Ephesians 2:19; Ephesians 3:8, 18; Ephesians 4:12; Ephesians 5:3; Ephesians6:18; Philippians 1:1; Philippians 4:22; Colossians 1:2, 4, 12, 26; 1 Thessalonians 3:13; 2 Thessalonians 1:10; 1 Timothy 5:10; Philemon 1:5, 7; Hebrews 6:10; Hebrew 13:24; Jude 1:3, 14; Revelation 5:8; Revelation 8:3, 4; Revelation 11:18; Revelation 13:7, 10; Revelation 14:12; Revelation 15:3; Revelation 16:6; Revelation 17:6; Revelation 18:24; Revelation 19:8; Revelation 20:9.

part of *"a royal priesthood."*[115] For we are the children of God,[116] cloaked in His righteousness through the substitutionary sacrifice of His Son, our Lord Jesus Christ. We are not to neglect the gathering of the saints!

With that said, let us also remember our future success and eternal life with God is not dependent on what church we belong to, or whether we even go to church. It is not dependent on what religion we belong to, or don't belong to for that matter. And it is not dependent on how many Christian friends we gather with. It is, however, entirely dependent on our personal relationship with God. The heart of the matter is this: Do you believe Jesus Christ is your Lord and Saviour? The truth is this: Unless you believe, nothing in these pages will matter in the long run. If you do not believe, Christ still loves you, and He cares for you, but you cannot claim a personal relationship with Him, and you cannot claim Him as a friend or Him your friend.[117] Nor can you claim His

---

[113] Genesis 7:1; Genesis 18:23, 24, 25, 26, 28;Genesis 38:26; Exodus 23:8; Numbers 23:10; Deuteronomy 16:19; Deuteronomy 25:1; 1 Samuel 24:17; 2 Samuel 4:11; 1 Kings 2:32; 1 Kings 8:32; 2 Kings 10:9; 2 Chronicles 6:23; Job 9:15; Job 17:9; Job 22:19; Job 23:7; Job 34:5; Job 35:7; Job 36:7; Job 40:8; Psalm 1:5, 6; Psalm 5:12; Psalm 7:11; Psalm 11:3, 5, 7; Psalm 14:5; Psalm 19:9; Psalm 31:18; Psalm 32:11; Psalm 33:1; Psalm 34:15, 17, 19; Psalm 37:16, 17, 21, 25, 29, 30, 32, 39; Psalm 52:6; Psalm 55:22; Psalm 58:10, 11; Psalm 64:10; Psalm 68:3; Psalm 69:28; Psalm 72:7; Psalm 75:10; Psalm 92:12; Psalm 94:21; Psalm 97:11, 12; Psalm 107:42; Psalm 112:4, 6; Psalm 118:20; Psalm 125:3; Psalm 140:13; Psalm 146:8; Proverbs 2:7, 20; Proverbs 3:32; Proverbs 10:3, 11, 16, 21, 24, 25, 28, 30, 32; Proverbs 11:8, 10, 21, 23, 28, 30, 31; Proverbs 12:3, 5, 7, 10, 12; Proverbs 12:26; Proverbs 13:5, 9, 21, 25; Proverbs 14:9, 19, 32; Proverbs 15:6; et al.

[114] Exodus 22:31; Exodus 29:33; Leviticus 11:44, 45; Leviticus 19:2; Leviticus 20:7, 26; Leviticus 21:6, 8; Leviticus 27:14; Numbers 6:5, 8; Numbers 15:40; Numbers 16:3, 5, 7; Deuteronomy 7:6; Deuteronomy 14:12, 21; Deuteronomy 26:19; Deuteronomy 28:9; 2 Kings 4:9; et al.

[115] 1 Peter 2:9.

[116] Matthew 5:9; Luke 20:36; Romans 8:16; 1 John 3:10; 1 John 5:2.

[117] John 15:14-15.

many promises for your personal growth and success, and eternal life with Him.

Being a *"believer"* means accepting Jesus Christ as your Lord and Saviour. And as such, Jesus says to us in John 15:14, *"Ye are my friends, if ye do whatsoever I command you."* Can you imagine that? The Creator of heaven and earth, and the entire universe, calls us *"friends!"* And we demonstrate our friendship with the Lord by following His commandments. One of those commandments is not to forsake the gathering of the saints.[118]

Gathering with fellow-believers in the Lord Jesus Christ serves several purposes, no purpose being greater than for the glory of God. We gather together to worship God, to edify one another with the gifts that God has bestowed on each believer, to lift the countenance of friends, to carry out the Great Commission with the support of a friend or friends, to learn the burdens and praises of our brothers and sisters in Christ, and pray for them, and to build and strengthen the body of Christ. *"For God is not the author of confusion,"* we read in 1 Corinthians 14:33, *"but of peace, as in all the churches of the saints."* We gather with fellow-believers because the Lord Jesus Christ calls on us to do so! You are needed!

Make no mistake about it, the future of America is in the hands of this gathering of the saints! Never underestimate the power of prayer and the collective influence of a righteous people on a holy God. Friends, there is a reason God gives us insight into His holy nature throughout Scripture. *"If my people,"* says the Lord God in 2 Chronicles 7:14, *"which are called by my name, shall humble themselves, and pray, and seek my*

---

[118] Hebrews 10:25.

face, and turn from their wicked ways; then will I hear from heaven, and will forgive their sin, and will heal their land." He hears and answers the prayers of His people individually and collectively when they gather and pray for His hand on their lives and the affairs of their nation.

Know the will of God! He has a plan and a purpose especially for you! He loves you unconditionally! And He delights in your prayers, and your desire to have a closer, more personal relationship with Him through His Son! Living your life with and for God, where all things are possible, is living a life of Faith!

Do not neglect the gathering of the saints!

~~~~~~~~~~

"These things I have spoken unto you, that in me ye might have peace. In the world ye shall have tribulation: but be of good cheer; I have overcome the world."

~ John 16:33

Chapter 15

We are the Sons of God

"For as many as are led by the Spirit of God, they are the sons of God."

~ Romans 8:14

"Do all things without murmurings and disputings:
That ye may be blameless and harmless, the sons of God,
without rebuke, in the midst of a crooked and perverse nation,
among whom ye shine as lights in the world;
Holding forth the word of life; that I may rejoice in the day of Christ,
that I have not run in vain, neither laboured in vain."

~ Philippians 2:14-16

Romans 1:17 says, *"For therein is the righteousness of God revealed from faith to faith: as it is written, The just shall live by faith."* These are powerful words! Know they were meant for you!

To be a Christian is special! It is to be led by the Holy Spirit, walking in Truth, conforming to the image of Christ Jesus, and having an ongoing desire to do the will of God. 1 Peter 2:9-10 states, *"⁹But ye are a chosen generation, a royal priesthood, an holy nation, a peculiar people; that ye should shew forth the praises of him who hath called you out of darkness into his marvellous light; ¹⁰Which in time past were not a people, but are now the people of God: which had not obtained mercy, but now have obtained mercy."*

The Word of God identifies believers as *"the sons of God,"*[119] which has deep and profound meaning when we realize Jesus was the Son of God. We are part of what Holy Scripture calls *"a royal priesthood,"*[120] *"saints"*[121] and *"righteous"*[122] and *"holy."*[123] For we are the children of God,[124] cloaked in His righteousness through the substitutionary sacrifice of His Son, our Lord Jesus Christ.

---

[119] Romans 8:14; Philippians 2:14-16.

[120] 1 Peter 2:9.

[121] 1 Samuel 2:9; 2 Chronicles 6:41; Psalm 16:3; Psalm 30:4; Psalm 31:23; Psalm 34:9; Psalm 37:28; Psalm 50:5; Psalm 52:9; Psalm 85:8; Psalm 89:5, 7; Psalm 97:10; Psalm 116:15; Psalm 132:9, 16; Psalm 145:10; Psalm 148:14; Psalm 149:1, 5, 9; Daniel 7:18, 21, 22, 25, 27; Hosea 11:12; Zechariah 14:5; Matthew 27:52; Acts 9:13, 32, 41; Acts 26:10; Romans 1:7; Romans 8:27; Romans 12:13; Romans 15:25, 26, 31; Romans 16:2, 15; 1 Corinthians 1:2; I Corinthians 6:1, 2; 1 Corinthians 14:33; 1 Corinthians 16:1, 15; 2 Corinthians 1:1; 2 Corinthians 8:4; 2 Corinthians 9:1, 12; 2 Corinthians 13:13; Ephesians 1:1, 15, 18; Ephesians 2:19; Ephesians 3:8, 18; Ephesians 4:12; Ephesians 5:3; Ephesians6:18; Philippians 1:1; Philippians 4:22; Colossians 1:2, 4, 12, 26; 1 Thessalonians 3:13; 2 Thessalonians 1:10; 1 Timothy 5:10; Philemon 1:5, 7; Hebrews 6:10; Hebrew 13:24; Jude 1:3, 14; Revelation 5:8; Revelation 8:3, 4; Revelation 11:18; Revelation 13:7, 10; Revelation 14:12; Revelation 15:3; Revelation 16:6; Revelation 17:6; Revelation 18:24; Revelation 19:8; Revelation 20:9.

[122] Genesis 7:1; Genesis 18:23, 24, 25, 26, 28;Genesis 38:26; Exodus 23:8; Numbers 23:10; Deuteronomy 16:19; Deuteronomy 25:1; 1 Samuel 24:17; 2 Samuel 4:11; 1 Kings 2:32; 1 Kings 8:32; 2 Kings 10:9; 2 Chronicles 6:23; Job 9:15; Job 17:9; Job 22:19; Job 23:7; Job 34:5; Job 35:7; Job 36:7; Job 40:8; Psalm 1:5, 6; Psalm 5:12; Psalm 7:11; Psalm 11:3, 5, 7; Psalm 14:5; Psalm 19:9; Psalm 31:18; Psalm 32:11; Psalm 33:1; Psalm 34:15, 17, 19; Psalm 37:16, 17, 21, 25, 29, 30, 32, 39; Psalm 52:6; Psalm 55:22; Psalm 58:10, 11; Psalm 64:10; Psalm 68:3; Psalm 69:28; Psalm 72:7; Psalm 75:10; Psalm 92:12; Psalm 94:21; Psalm 97:11, 12; Psalm 107:42; Psalm 112:4, 6; Psalm 118:20; Psalm 125:3; Psalm 140:13; Psalm 146:8; Proverbs 2:7, 20; Proverbs 3:32; Proverbs 10:3, 11, 16, 21, 24, 25, 28, 30, 32; Proverbs 11:8, 10, 21, 23, 28, 30, 31; Proverbs 12:3, 5, 7, 10, 12; Proverbs 12:26; Proverbs 13:5, 9, 21, 25; Proverbs 14:9, 19, 32; Proverbs 15:6; et al.

[123] Exodus 22:31; Exodus 29:33; Leviticus 11:44, 45; Leviticus 19:2; Leviticus 20:7, 26; Leviticus 21:6, 8; Leviticus 27:14; Numbers 6:5, 8; Numbers 15:40; Numbers 16:3, 5, 7; Deuteronomy 7:6; Deuteronomy 14:12, 21; Deuteronomy 26:19; Deuteronomy 28:9; 2 Kings 4:9; et al.

[124] Matthew 5:9; Luke 20:36; Romans 8:16; 1 John 3:10; 1 John 5:2.

But we live in a world that seeks to diminish the power and impact of Christ, and deceive those who follow Him as Lord. I have even heard self-professed Christians say, *"I am just a poor sinner,"* or *"I'm only human, of course I still sin!"* But how can that be, especially if we know the Word of God?

We who believe on the Lord Christ Jesus are *"saved,"* there is no condemnation.[125] In Psalm 103:12, we read, *"As far as the east is from the west, so far hath he removed our transgressions from us."* God shares His level of forgiveness in Hebrews 10:17-18, when He states, *"17And their sins and iniquities will I remember no more. 18Now where remission of these is, there is no more offering for sin."* Moreover, Romans 6:14 declares, *"For sin shall not have dominion over you: for ye are not under the law, but under grace."* Sin has no place in the life of a Christian, because we dwell in a state of grace. *"But now being made free from sin, and become servants to God, ye have your fruit unto holiness, and the end everlasting life,"* notes the apostle Paul in Romans 6:22. And he continues in Romans 6:23, *"For the wages of sin is death; but the gift of God is eternal life through Jesus Christ our Lord."* And lest there be any doubt, 1 John 3:9 declares, *"Whosoever is born of God doth not commit sin; for his seed remaineth in him: and he cannot sin, because he is born of God."* This is why Jesus could heal and rescue those oppressed during His ministry on earth, and affirmatively tell them, *"Sin no more."*[126] He meant it!

Sin does not exist in a state of grace. Christians might transgress and drift from the will of God, but we do not sin. Sin separates us from God, and if we still sin, then we would

---

[125] Romans 8:1, *"There is therefore **now** no condemnation to them which are in Christ Jesus, who walk **not** after the flesh, but after the Spirit."*

[126] John 5:14, *"Afterward Jesus findeth him in the temple, and said unto him, Behold, thou art made whole: **sin no more**, lest a worse thing come unto thee.";* John 8:11, *"She said, No man, Lord. And Jesus said unto her, Neither do I condemn thee: go, and **sin no more**."*

become separated from God and lose our salvation every time we sin. But the truth is: You cannot lose your salvation! You are either saved or a sinner, under grace or under the law, a son of God or a son of perdition,[127] found by God or lost and destined for hell. Do not be distracted by false doctrine and the wiles of the devil. Know the Truth!

And if you are one of the few who believe you actually could lose your salvation, you are wrong, and you need to study Holy Scripture. Jesus clearly said, *"I will never leave thee, nor forsake thee."*[128] Note the following exchange in John 10:24-29:

> [24] Then came the Jews round about him, and said unto him, How long dost thou make us to doubt? If thou be the Christ, tell us plainly.

> [25] Jesus answered them, I told you, and ye believed not: the works that I do in my Father's name, they bear witness of me.

> [26] But ye believe not, because ye are not of my sheep, as I said unto you.

> [27] My sheep hear my voice, and I know them, and they follow me:

> [28] And I give unto them eternal life; and they shall never perish, neither shall any man pluck them out of my hand.

> [29] My Father, which gave them me, is greater than all; and no man is able to pluck them out of my Father's hand.

---

[127] John 17:12; Philippians 1:28; 2 Thessalonians 2:3; 1 Timothy 6:9; Hebrews 10:39; 2 Peter 3:7; Revelation 17:8, 11.
[128] Hebrews 13:5.

Note Jesus says of the saved, *"neither shall any man pluck them out of my hand"*[129] and *"no man is able to pluck them out of my Father's hand."*[130] This means: Once saved = Always saved! That is the promise of God! Count on it!

We live in an age that would promote hopelessness and condemnation. Live your life with faith, hope, and love!

We also live in a time when many claim they can *"save"* themselves by leading a relatively good life. *"After all,"* they claim, *"I didn't kill anybody!"* Salvation is, as Ephesians 2:9 tells us, *"Not of works, lest any man should boast."* While most did not kill anyone, they are ignorant of the righteousness of God, His laws, and His Word. Otherwise, they would understand that salvation is not a work of man, lest any man boast,[131] but a gift from God,[132] received only by the saving grace of our Lord.[133]

Even when we read the express words of Jesus, some will change them to suit their agenda. This is false doctrine. For example, in John 15:16, Jesus states, *"Ye have not chosen me, but I have chosen you, and ordained you, that ye should go and bring forth fruit, and that your fruit should remain: that whatsoever ye shall ask of the Father in my name, he may give it you."* However, I have heard many say, *"I chose to accept Christ."* This is not so, for as we read in Romans 3:11, *"There is none that understandeth, there is none that seeketh after God."* No one seeks God on their own accord. It is the work of the Holy Spirit that draws men to the free gift of God.

---

[129] John 10:28.
[130] John 10:29.
[131] Ephesians 2:9.
[132] Romans 5:15.
[133] Romans 5:17.

And herein we find the mission of the sons of God. We are led by the Holy Spirit to shine as light upon a lost and dying world. Not to live in condemnation or doubt, but in faith and hope and love. We are to know Truth, and to conform to the image of our Saviour and Lord, and seek that which is lost. To echo the call of repentance to a lost and dying world, for the kingdom of God is at hand. We are to answer the call of the Great Commission, and do the will of God. This is the quest of the sons of God.

~~~~~~~~~~

"So shall my word be that goeth forth out of my mouth:
it shall not return unto me void, but it shall accomplish that which I please,
and it shall prosper in the thing whereto I sent it."

~ *Isaiah 55:11*

Chapter 16

Choose Life, Not Death

"But whoso shall offend one of these little ones which believe in me,
it were better for him that a millstone were hanged about his neck,
and that he were drowned in the depth of the sea."

~ Matthew 18:6

"Thou shalt not kill."

~ Exodus 20:13

"Lo, children are an heritage of the LORD:
and the fruit of the womb is his reward."

~ Psalm 127:3

"Before I formed thee in the belly I knew thee;
and before thou camest forth out of the womb I sanctified thee,
and I ordained thee a prophet unto the nations."

~ Jeremiah 1:5

Perhaps the most divisive *"social issue"* of our time is the issue of abortion, that is, the killing of helpless babies. There is one side, which calls it *"choice,"* and *"a woman's right."* And then there are those who call it *"wrong"* and *"murder,"* that is, the intentional taking of a life of another human being with malice aforethought. In the law, *"malice"* is an evil mind, and the word *"aforethought"* connotes a thought out plan. In my opinion, abortion is murder.

Children are a gift of God. Something God cherishes, and warns against harming in His Word. They are created in His image, for His purpose. But as a society we have ignored the admonishments of God, and choose death for these little ones. As Jesus shares in Matthew 25:40, *"Verily I say unto you, Inasmuch as ye have done it unto one of the least of these my brethren, ye have done it unto me."*

I am reminder of a story I once heard. It went like this: A liberal person frustrated with the state of affairs of the world shouts from rooftop at God: *"How can I believe in you? You allow pain and suffering! You see the afflictions of your children and you do nothing! People around the world are dying from starvation and disease! Why didn't you do something!?"*

And God answered: *"My child, I did do something! I sent brilliant people with minds to cure hunger and disease---but you aborted them!"*

A simple story, but a powerful message! We need to understand that God is perfect, and humans who rely on their own understandings and emotions are fallible. We need to rely on God, and have faith in Him, and His ways and plans, all of which are revealed in Holy Scripture. Read it! And see the world through God's eyes, and remember what he said in Matthew 18:6, *"But whoso shall offend one of these little ones which believe in me, it were better for him that a millstone were hanged about his neck, and that he were drowned in the depth of the sea."* Strong words, none of which are to be taken lightly!

Believe me, I understand the arguments, and I will not belabor the points or sugarcoat them. Abortion is inconsistent with the Word of God.[134] If you are a believer who knows the

---

[134] Exodus 20:13; Deuteronomy 5:17; Matthew 5:21; Romans 13:9.

Word of God, then you know this truth. A baby in the womb of his or her mother is not an enemy soldier on the battlefield or a criminal who committed a capital offense and was found guilty by a jury of his or her peers. A baby is an innocent human being, made in the image of God. If you are a believer who had an abortion, you are not under condemnation. God loves you, unconditionally, and His mercy is great. If you know of someone contemplating abortion, share the Truth of God's Word. Tell them to *"Choose Life!"* And always remember God's wonderful commentary on the effect of His Word in Isaiah 55:11, *"So shall my word be that goeth forth out of my mouth: it shall not return unto me void, but it shall accomplish that which I please, and it shall prosper in the thing whereto I sent it."* We all benefit and prosper with the knowledge of, and adherence to, the Word of God!

If you are a follower of the Lord Jesus Christ, and know His Word, there is no debate. Treat others as you would have them treat you. Choose Life, not death!

~~~~~~~~~

"Thou shalt not kill."

~ Exodus 20:13

"And the light shineth in darkness; and the darkness comprehended it not."

~ John 1:5

"For God so loved the world, that he gave his only begotten Son, that whosoever believeth in him should not perish, but have everlasting life."

~ John 3:16

Conclusion

Fear God, & Keep His Commandments

*"And in that day ye shall ask me nothing. Verily, verily, I say unto you,
Whatsoever ye shall ask the Father in my name, he will give it you.
Hitherto have ye asked nothing in my name:
ask, and ye shall receive, that your joy may be full."*

~ John 16:23-24

*"Let us hear the conclusion of the whole matter:
Fear God, and keep his commandments:
for this is the whole duty of man."*

~ Ecclesiastes 12:13

So here we are, at the conclusion of this book, a simple walk, if you will. But the great journey lay ahead. A journey of discovery and abundance, a journey of developing faith in you --- a mustard seed-size amount of faith, and more --- and achieving the *"impossible"* in the eyes of men! This is true for you and your marriage! This is a promise of God! Just one of many He promises to His friends! For as Jesus said, *"I am come that they might have life, and that they might have it more abundantly."*[135] Know in your heart He was talking about you!

Scripture tells us, *"Faith is the substance of things hoped for,*

---

[135] John 10:10.

the evidence of things not seen."[136]   And Scripture goes on to state, "But without faith it is impossible to please him: for he that cometh to God must believe that he is, and that he is a rewarder of them that diligently seek him."[137] But where does this faith come from? Well, Scripture has an answer to this as well: "So then faith cometh by hearing, and hearing by the word of God."[138]

With this in mind, it is important to note that this book will not give you faith. It is a work about the power of God in your life through faith in Him. If you and your spouse seek faith, seek the Word of God. And there is no greater authority on His Word than the Holy Bible. It also needs to be said that we can hear the Word of God through godly counsel from preachers and fellow-believers. You can even learn some of His Word through this work, but I caution you to compare whatever you read here, or hear from other men and women, with what is written in the Holy Bible, and always defer to what the Holy Bible teaches. Again, the Holy Bible is the authority on Truth. I speak on this subject throughout this work, with particular focus in latter chapters on putting on the full armour of God and the foundations of the Faith.

In this age of cynicism, where we are taught to question all traditional notions of duty, honor, country … and our Creator. We are expected to embrace the "wisdom" of men, and doubt the existence of God and His interaction with us in our lives. With that said, it is a difficult thing to walk in optimism, faith and hope. From the moment we leave the innocence of childhood, we are exposed to a myriad of shattering realities. The world tells us many things: People lie. They deceive. They make bold pronouncements that shake

---

[136] Hebrews 11:1.
[137] Hebrews 11:6.
[138] Romans 10:17.

our faith. They betray and they forsake one another for selfish reasons, personal gain and ambition. And, among other things, love fails.

But there is an alternative. A way to live life optimistically, dwelling on good things, and with the virtues of faith, hope, and love at the forefront. This is living life more abundantly. This is living a life of Faith. And that is what this book is all about. It is a guide that points the way to Truth, and in that Truth, an anchor that grounds us to an immovable foundation.

Is this too good to be true? No! Not if you have Faith, and Hope, and most of all, Love. But it all starts with a leap of faith, like that of a little child. As Jesus says in Mark 10:15, *"Verily I say unto you, Whosoever shall not receive the kingdom of God as a little child shall in no wise enter therein."* Rekindle the wonderful hope you had as a child: Believe! And be willing to accept help in this difficult journey we call Life. I believe that is why YOU are reading this book at this very moment! It is not by chance or happenstance! YOU were meant to be learning this Truth! Proverbs 8:33 states, *"Hear instruction, and be wise, and refuse it not."* This is key! And Proverbs 9:9 builds on this proposition by stating, *"Give instruction to a wise man, and he will be yet wiser: teach a just man, and he will increase in learning."* So boldly accept godly instruction! Be wise! And learn!

Accept Truth, even when the world tells you it may not be reasonable. Men are fallible, but God is not. Listen to the Word of God, and the godly counsel of those who walk with God and know His Word. Remember God's admonishment in Proverbs 12:15, *"The way of a fool is right in his own eyes: but he that hearkeneth unto counsel is wise."* Do not be a fool, and do not be afraid or embarrassed. Be of great joy! And embrace the proposition that there is more to life than the brief shining moment we spend on earth.

In Isaiah 41:10, we read:

> [10] Do not fear, for I am with you; Do not anxiously look about you, for I am your God. I will strengthen you, surely I will help you, Surely I will uphold you with My righteous right hand. [NASB]

So there is no mistake, and no sense of being deceived, let me make this perfectly clear: This is a book about the love of God, and the evil of Divorce and the industry spawned of Satan to perpetuate that evil. It is an offense to God and grieves the Holy Spirit. This is a book about how you and your family can benefit from God's unconditional love and the promises He makes to YOU. As Francis Bacon said, *"Knowledge is power."*

This is a work about the power of God through you in Faith. Faith is not fearful or anxious. The Bible is replete with admonishments from God for you and me to *fear not*[139] and to be *anxious for nothing*.[140] He says these words for a reason. And as 2 Timothy 1:7 reminds us, *"For God hath not given us the spirit of fear; but of power, and of love, and of a sound mind."* Know that whatever problems, difficulties or challenges you face, no matter how dire they may seem, God can and will help you. Victory is within your grasp, and it is not by chance you are reading these very words. God has a purpose and a plan for you! My friends, I speak from personal experience.

---

[139] Genesis 15:1, 21:17, 26:24, 35:17, 43:23, 46:3, 50:21; Exodus 14:13, 20:20; Numbers 1:34; Deuteronomy 1:21, 3:2, 3:22, 20:3, 31:6, 31:8; Joshua 8:1, 10:25; Judges 4:18, 6:10, 6:23; Ruth 3:11; 1 Samuel 12:20, 22:23, 23:17; 2 Samuel 9:7, 13:28; 1 Kings 17:13; 2 Kings

Satan is a formidable foe. The prince of darkness even tempted our Lord on many occasions. So it is little wonder that he will seek to tempt you, your spouse, if you are married, your family, and your friends. I know because he worked his wiles on me, my wife, my children, and my friends and associates. It is what he does. And although he achieved limited successes, he is destined to lose the war, because it is God's law that good shall overcome evil.[141]

But no matter where you are in life, this book has something for you! You may be hurting from the loss of a loved one or in great despair, feeling hopeless. You may be searching for personal growth or success, or both. You may already be successful. You may be part of what the world calls the *"underprivileged"* or the *"middle class"* or the *"top 1%."* You may be unemployed, working, a student, retired, or a homemaker. You may be a sinner or saved, a sales person on the floor of a local department store or a member of the clergy. It does not matter. You will be better off for having read this book, because it holds within these pages a timeless Truth. If you read this book and apply the principles contained herein, you will experience a changed life!

As an attorney and counselor at law, former law school professor and judge, I have spent a significant amount of my life studying, teaching, and applying the Law. In a very meaningful way, this book is about the Law , but it is also

---

6:16, 17:35, 17:37, 17:38, 25:24; 1 Chronicles 28:20; 2 Chronicles 20:17; Job 11:15; Psalm 27:3, 56:4, 118:6; Proverbs 3:25; Isaiah 7:4, 8:12, 35:4, 41:10, 41:13, 41:14, 43:1, 43:5, 44:2, 44:8, 51:7, 54:4, 54:14; Jeremiah 40:9, 46:27, 46:28; Lamentations 3:57; Ezekiel 3:9; Daniel 10:12, 10:19; Joel 2:21; Zephaniah 3:16; Haggai 2:5; Zechariah 8:13, 8:15; Matthew 1:20, 10:26, 10:28, 10:31, 28:5; Luke 1:13, 1:30, 2:10, 5:10, 8:50, 12:7, 12:32; John 12:15; Acts 27:24; 2 Timothy 1:7; Hebrews 13:6; 1 John 4:18; Revelation 1:17.

[140] Isaiah 41:10; Jeremiah 17:8; Philippians 4:6.

[141] 1 John 3:8, et al.

about Grace. The former was handed down through Moses in the Ten Commandments,[142] and established the very foundation of our current civil and criminal laws. *"Thou shalt not kill."*[143] *"Thou shalt not commit adultery."*[144] *"Thou shalt not steal."*[145] *"Thou shalt not bear false witness against thy neighbor."*[146] These are each part of the Ten Commandments, and they are obvious statutes we can readily find in the legal codes of our modern civilization. But in many ways, they are statutes that condemn, being punishable under the Law when violated. I dare say you could not find a human being alive on our planet that has not been in violation of at least one of these commandments under the law during his or her lifetime.

However, Grace is another matter. It is a gift from God.[147] And Grace is a state separate from and above the Law. Grace allows us to live with the protection and power of God, whereas only perfect adherence to the Law allows us to live a life free of prosecution. Perfection is an exceedingly high standard, and any transgression or sin under the law is punishable. In fact, perfection is too high a standard for man to achieve without God, as we suffer from a sin nature.[148] In His Word, God states:

> [23] For all have sinned, and come short of the glory of God;
>
> [24] Being justified freely by his grace through the redemption that is in Christ Jesus:

---

[142] Exodus 34:28.
[143] Exodus 20:13.
[144] Exodus 20:14.
[145] Exodus 20:15.
[146] Exodus 20:16.
[147] Romans 5:15.
[148] Romans 3:23.

25 Whom God hath set forth to be a propitiation through faith in his blood, to declare his righteousness for the remission of sins that are past, through the forbearance of God;

26 To declare, I say, at this time his righteousness: that he might be just, and the justifier of him which believeth in Jesus. [Romans 3:23-26]

In effect, there are two states of being: Under the Law or under Grace. Living under the Law is a state of being that condemns you once you sin,[149] but living under Grace removes the sin that would separate us from God.[150] *"For sin shall not have dominion over you,"* states Roman 6:14, *"for ye are not under the law, but under grace."* And Galatians 2:21 states, *"for if righteousness come by the law, then Christ is dead in vain."* The Lord Jesus Christ did not die in vain! *"For the law was given by Moses,"* John 1:17 enlightens us, *"but grace and the truth came by Jesus Christ."*

Finally, it is important to note that Grace does not relieve us from our duty to obey the Law, that being, the Commandments of God and the laws of governments, as long as the latter do not conflict with the Word of God. In John 14:15, Jesus says, *"If ye love me, keep my commandments."* This is not an option, it is a command. We are to obey His commandments. These include the original Ten and all others brought forth in Holy Scripture through guidance from the Holy Spirit. And Jesus further commanded our respect and obedience for man-made law in Matthew 22:21, when He said, *"Render therefore unto Caesar the things which are Caesar's; and*

---

[149] Ezekiel 18:4.
[150] Romans 6:23.

unto God the things that are God's."[151]

While it may seem strange to some to have an attorney write a book on the evil of Divorce and the promises of God, think about it in context of the Holy Bible. The apostle Paul was originally a strict advocate of the Law. He even stood by in support of those that stoned to Stephen, the first Christian martyr, to death.[152] Paul was an enemy of the fledgling Christian church, but it was God's plan for his life that he should be a powerful evangelist of the Gospel of Jesus Christ. And he was. Paul answered God's call to preach the Word of God, and his impact is still felt today.

Not that I am in any way putting myself in Paul's league, I am not. I consider myself a mere babe in the study of God's Word, for it contains within its pages the very sum total of all knowledge and understanding for the benefit of all mankind. In the Holy Bible is the answer to all, and I do mean all, the problems and challenges facing man. It has all the answers you will ever need to be successful and grow and do the *"impossible."* In Micah 6:8 we read, *"He hath shewed thee, O man, what is good; and what doth the* LORD *require of thee, but to do justly, and to love mercy, and to walk humbly with thy God?"* I am learning new things every day, and in my walk of faith and understanding, I understand that I have a privilege and a duty to share what I have learned. It is my hope that you will do this as well.

In this work, my focus is on the fact that we are all lost and powerless without God in our lives. Faith in God is the answer! And the beauty of this is that God accepts us just as we are. He then does a work in our lives. In my life, I find the

---

[151] *See also* Mark 12:17 & Luke 20:25.
[152] Acts 7:58 - 8:1.

more I grow in my walk with the Lord, the more I am compelled to share His life-changing Gospel. I learn, and I share. And I find time after time this simple sharing does wonders in the lives of friends and associates who struggle with the same trials and challenges I do. This sharing is something Scripture commands us to do.[153] None of us are called to take this walk of faith alone.

This book is important for several compelling reasons. It is a glimpse of God's unconditional love, and His acceptance of you just as you are! Like Paul, it doesn't matter what you did in your past. *"Therefore if any man be in Christ, he is a new creature,"* writes Paul in 2 Corinthians 5:17, *"old things are passed away; behold, all things are become new."* This is the power of the Gospel of Jesus Christ. It is life-changing!

This book explains why the veil that separated man from God was torn at that moment on the cross.[154] This was the point in history that gave men the ability to do the impossible through the power of God available to them through Faith. The power to move mountains is still there and available to YOU! And in that context, Divorce in NEVER the right answer.

And this is a book that encourages, provides hope, and gives meaning to life, because it is a commentary on the Gospel. I have heard it said by one friend in the faith that the Gospel is best defined as: *"The Good News of Jesus Christ and His offer of salvation through His death, burial, and resurrection, that we receive through faith."*[155]

---

[153] Hebrews 10:13; Hebrews 10:25; Romans 14:19; 1 Corinthians 14:26; 2 Corinthians 12:19; Ephesians 4:12; Ephesians 4:16; Ephesians 4:29; 1 Thessalonians 5:11; 1 Timothy 1:4.
[154] Matthew 27:50-54.
[155] Dr. Charles F. Stanley, Senior Pastor, First Baptist Church of Atlanta, 2012.

It is my prayer that you are reading this book because you are seeking God's hand upon your life, perhaps in your marriage. Alternatively, perhaps you are reading this book because someone thought well enough of you to share the essence of this Good News with you. 1 Peter 4:10 tells us, *"As every man hath received the gift, even so minister the same one to another, as good stewards of the manifold grace of God."* Now that is living life at its very best!

As I mentioned earlier, I learn and I share. It is my hope that you will do the same. And as I continue to learn, I am persuaded that this book is yet another on the power of God, a work in progress: One of many on the subject, as I do not intend to stagnate in my walk or my life. I have pledged to learn every day and share the Good News of the Kingdom of God.

I began this book by telling you what the world thinks about many things, including Marriage and Love. But let me cut to the chase, and conclude this passage on a positive note. After all, that is what this work is all about. Let me tell you what God says about Love:

> [4] Love is patient, love is kind and is not jealous; love does not brag and is not arrogant,

> [5] does not act unbecomingly; it does not seek its own, is not provoked, does not take into account a wrong suffered,

> [6] does not rejoice in unrighteousness, but rejoices with the truth;

7 bears all things, believes all things, hopes all things, endures all things. [1 Corinthians 13:4-7, NASB]

Believe this about Marriage!

And now that we know about Love, let us apply what God shares in 1 John 4:7, *"Beloved, let us love one another: for love is of God; and every one that loveth is born of God, and knoweth God."* Know God! And trust the truth He exclaims in the very next verse of the previous reading in 1 Corinthians, *"Love never fails."*[156] My friends, believe, and *"receive the kingdom of God as a little child."*[157]

Behold the Kingdom of God ... and prepare ye the way to live life and the institution of marriage as God intended! And to the Prodigal Spouses out there, I say, as it is written, *"Arise and go"* to thy father God![158]

~~~~~~~~~~

"And the things that thou hast heard of me among many witnesses,
the same commit thou to faithful men, who shall be able to teach others also."

~ 2 Timothy 2:2

---

[156] 1 Corinthians 13:8, NASB.
[157] Mark 10:15.
[158] Luke 15:18.

Compendium

The Promises of God

"For all the promises of God in him are yea,
and in him Amen, unto the glory of God by us."

~ 2 Corinthians 1:20

The Holy Bible is replete with the promises of God. They are foundations and anchors for your marriage. Know in your heart they are meant for YOU! What follows are just a few of my favorites, but you are strongly encouraged to discover the ones meant just for you in your walk of Faith. For those familiar with my writings, you know these references to Holy Scripture are a mainstay of my work, providing a lamp unto my feet, and a light unit my path.[159]

Favor

"For thou, LORD, wilt bless the righteous;
with favour wilt thou compass him as with a shield."

~ Psalm 5:12

---

[159] Psalm 119:105.

Unconditional Love

"The LORD hath appeared of old unto me, saying,
Yea, I have loved thee with an everlasting love:
therefore with lovingkindness have I drawn thee."

~ Jeremiah 31:3

Drawing Close to God

"Draw nigh to God, and he will draw nigh to you."

~ James 4:8

Companionship

"Let your conversation be without covetousness;
and be content with such things as ye have:
for he hath said, I will never leave thee, nor forsake thee."

~ Hebrews 5:13

Prayer

"Call unto me, and I will answer thee,
and show thee great and mighty things,
which thou knowest not."

~ Jeremiah 33:3

Friendship

"Ye are my friends, if ye do whatsoever I command you."

~ John 15:14

Provision

"But my God shall supply all your need
According to his riches in glory by Christ Jesus."

~ Philippians 4:19

Wisdom

"If any of you lack wisdom, let him ask of God, that giveth to
all men liberally, and upbraideth not;
and it shall be given him."

~ James 1:5

Protection

"For he shall give his angels charge over thee,
to keep thee in all thy ways."

~ Psalm 91:11

Peace

"And the peace of God, which passeth all understanding,
shall keep your hearts and minds through Christ Jesus."

~ Philippians 4:7

Joy

"Thou wilt shew me the path of life: in thy presence is fulness
of joy; at thy right hand there are pleasures for evermore."

~ Psalm 16:11

Strength

"I can do all things through Christ which strengtheneth me."

~ Philippians 4:13

Victory

"But thanks be to God,
which giveth us the victory through our Lord Jesus Christ."

~ 1 Corinthians 15:57

~~~~~~~~~~~

"Give, and it shall be given unto you; good measure, pressed down, and shaken together, and running over, shall men give into your bosom. For with the same measure that ye mete withal it shall be measured to you again."

~ Luke 6:38

"We have God's promise that what we give will be given back many times over, so let us go forth from here and rekindle the fire of our faith. Let our wisdom be vindicated by our deeds."

~ President Ronald Reagan
February 4, 1982

Biblical Passages

Strengthening Your Marriage

"So shall my word be that goeth forth out of my mouth:
it shall not return unto me void, but it shall accomplish that which I please,
and it shall prosper in the thing whereto I sent it."

~ Isaiah 55:11

2 Timothy 3:16-17 states, *"16All scripture is given by inspiration of God, and is profitable for doctrine, for reproof, for correction, for instruction in righteousness: 17That the man of God may be perfect, thoroughly furnished unto all good works."* Know with all of your heart, and soul, and mind, this was written for you! You and your marriage are special and important to God. Yes, the God who created the universe and made all things is personally interested in you, your marriage, and your future. Here is what God says: *"'For I know the plans that I have for you,' declares the Lord, 'plans for welfare and not for calamity to give you a future and a hope.'"*[160] He gave you and me the Word so that we might have a restored close and personal relationship with Him. He loves you! Believe in Him, and trust Him! His Word applies to you!

With this in mind, the remainder of this work is dedicated to heralding the Word of God as it is given from the mouth of God. It will not return void. It will accomplish what

---

[160] Jeremiah 29:11, NASB.

God wants. It will develop in you faith in the amount of a mustard seed ... and more! It will prosper you ... and your marriage! READ IT!

Whether you are afflicted with loneliness, poverty, grief, or just have questions about God and His plans for you, the following passages gleamed from Holy Scripture are proffered for your edification. They are not all-inclusive. They are but a glimpse into the Word of God on these topics. They are the pathway to building your faith! You are encouraged to read the Holy Bible every day, and walk in the light of His truth and for living in the power of God.

Do not fall for the naysayers who seek to discourage you. They say, *"The Bible is too difficult to read."* It is not! Rely on the promises of God in Matthew 7:7-8, *"[7]Ask and it will be given to you; seek and you will find; knock and the door will be opened to you. [8]For everyone who asks receives; the one who seeks finds; and to the one who knocks, the door will be opened."* Count on Him in the person of the Holy Spirit to guide you through Scripture, and to a closer, personal relationship with Him. This is the path to growing your Faith!

Seize this moment! Discover personal growth and the way to a successful life! James 4:8 promises, *"Draw nigh to God, and he will draw nigh to you."* Draw near to God!

~~~~~~~~~~

"So then faith cometh by hearing, and hearing by the word of God."

~ Romans 10:17

Passages On
Faith

"Faith is the substance of things hoped for,
the evidence of things not seen."

~ Hebrews 11:1

"If ye have faith as a grain of mustard seed, ye shall say unto
this mountain, Remove hence to yonder place; and it shall
remove; and nothing shall be impossible unto you."

~ Matthew 17:20

"But Jesus beheld them, and said unto them,
With men this is impossible;
but with God all things are possible."

~ Matthew 19:26

"That your faith should not stand in the wisdom of men,
but in the power of God."

~ 1 Corinthians 2:5

"But without faith it is impossible to please him:
for he that cometh to God must believe that he is,
and that he is a rewarder of them that diligently seek him."

~ Hebrews 11:6

"So then faith cometh by hearing,
and hearing by the word of God."

~ Romans 10:17

"For therein is the righteousness of God revealed from faith to
faith: as it is written, The just shall live by faith."

~ Romans 1:17

"Even so faith, if it hath not works, is dead, being alone."

~ James 2:17

"For as the body without the spirit is dead,
so faith without works is dead also."

~ James 2:26

~~~~~~~~~~

These passages are but a glimpse into the Word of God on this subject.
You are encouraged to read the Holy Bible every day,
and walk in the light of His truth …
to grow your Faith.

Passages On
God

"In the beginning God created the heaven and the earth."

~ Genesis 1:1

"In the beginning was the Word,
and the Word was with God, and the Word was God."

~ John 1:1

"Jesus Christ the same yesterday, and today, and forever."

~ Hebrews 13:8

"I am Alpha and Omega, the beginning and the ending, saith
the Lord, which is, and which was,
and which is to come, the Almighty."

~ Revelation 1:18

"Thy word is a lamp unto my feet, and a light unto my path."

~ Psalm 119:105

"Herein is love, not that we loved God, but that he loved us, and sent his Son to be the propitiation for our sins."

~ 1 John 4:10

"God is love;
and he that dwelleth in love dwelleth in God,
and God in him."

~ 1 John 4:16

"For unto you is born this day in the city of David a Saviour, which is Christ the Lord."

~ Luke 2:11

"In whose hand is the soul of every living thing, and the breath of all mankind."

~ Job 12:10

"For God so loved the world,
that he gave his only begotten Son,
that whosoever believeth in him should not perish,
but have everlasting life."

~ John 3:16

"Then spake Jesus again unto them, saying, I am the light of the world: he that followeth me shall not walk in darkness, but shall have the light of life."

~ John 8:12

"But Jesus beheld them, and said unto them,
With men this is impossible;
but with God all things are possible."

~Matthew 19:26

"The LORD on high is mightier than the noise of many waters,
yea, than the mighty waves of the sea."

~ Psalm 93:4

"He telleth the number of the stars;
he calleth them all by their names."

~ Psalm 147:4

"For there are three that bear record in heaven, the Father, the
Word, and the Holy Ghost: and these three are one."

~ 1 John 5:7

"Jesus saith unto him, I am the way, the truth, and the life: no
man cometh unto the Father, but by me."

~ John 14:6

"And I heard as it were the voice of a great multitude, and as
the voice of many waters, and as the voice of mighty
thunderings, saying, Alleluia:
for the Lord God omnipotent reigneth."

~ Revelation 19:6

"I Jesus have sent mine angel to testify unto you these things in the churches. I am the root and the offspring of David, and the bright and morning star."

~ Revelation 22:16

~~~~~~~~~~

These passages are but a glimpse into the Word of God on this subject.
You are encouraged to read the Holy Bible every day,
and walk in the light of His truth ...
to grow your Faith.

Passages On
You

"For God so loved the world,
that he gave his only begotten Son,
that whosoever believeth in him should not perish,
but have everlasting life."

~ John 3:16

"Whether therefore ye eat, or drink, or whatsoever ye do,
do all to the glory of God."

~ Psalm 37:23

"But my God shall supply all your need
According to his riches in glory by Christ Jesus."

~ Philippians 4:19

"Ye are the light of the world.
A city that is set on an hill cannot be hid.
Neither do men light a candle,
and put it under a bushel, but on a candlestick;
and it giveth light unto all that are in the house.
Let your light so shine before men, that they may see your
good works, and glorify your Father which is in heaven."

~ Matthew 5:14-16

"But the very hairs of your head are all numbered.
Fear ye not therefore,
ye are of more value than many sparrows."

~ Matthew 10:30-31

"Before I formed thee in the belly I knew thee;
and before thou camest forth out of the womb
I sanctified thee,
and I ordained thee a prophet unto the nations."

~ Jeremiah 1:5

"Take fast hold of instruction; let her not go:
keep her; for she is thy life."

~ Proverbs 4:13

"Hear counsel, and receive instruction,
that thou mayest be wise in thy latter end."

~ Proverbs 19:20

"But we are bound to give thanks alway to God for you,
brethren beloved of the Lord, because God hath from the
beginning chosen you to salvation through sanctification of
the Spirit and belief of the truth:
Whereunto he called you by our gospel,
to the obtaining of the glory of our Lord Jesus Christ.
Therefore, brethren, stand fast, and hold the traditions
which ye have been taught, whether by word, or our epistle."

~ 2 Thessalonians 2:13-15

"Let us hear the conclusion of the whole matter:
Fear God, and keep his commandments:
for this is the whole duty of man."

~ Ecclesiastes 12:13

~~~~~~~~~~

These passages are but a glimpse into the Word of God on this subject.
You are encouraged to read the Holy Bible every day,
and walk in the light of His truth ...
to grow your Faith.

Passages On
Wisdom

"For where envying and strife is,
there is confusion and every evil work.
But the wisdom that is from above is first pure, then
peaceable, gentle, and easy to be intreated, full of mercy and
good fruits, without partiality, and without hypocrisy."

~ James 3:16-17

"The fear of the LORD is the beginning of wisdom: and the
knowledge of the holy is understanding."

~ Proverbs 9:10

"Wise men lay up knowledge:
but the mouth of the foolish is near destruction."

~ Proverbs 10:14

"So shall the knowledge of wisdom be unto thy soul:
when thou hast found it, then there shall be a reward,
and thy expectation shall not be cut off."

~ Proverbs 24:14

"But we speak the wisdom of God in a mystery,
even the hidden wisdom, which God ordained
before the world unto our glory:
Which none of the princes of this world knew:
for had they known it, they would
not have crucified the Lord of glory.
But as it is written, Eye hath not seen, nor ear heard,
neither have entered into the heart of man,
the things which God hath prepared for them that love him."

~ 1 Corinthians 2:7-9

"Happy is the man that findeth wisdom,
and the man that getteth understanding.
For the merchandise of it is better than the merchandise of
silver, and the gain thereof than fine gold."

~ Proverbs 3:13-14

"Buy the truth, and sell it not;
also wisdom, and instruction, and understanding."

~ Proverbs 23:23

"For wisdom is a defence, and money is a defence:
but the excellency of knowledge is,
that wisdom giveth life to them that have it."

~ Ecclesiastes 7:12

"Wisdom strengtheneth the wise more than ten mighty men
which are in the city."

~ Ecclesiastes 7:19

"For whoso findeth me [Wisdom] findeth life,
and shall obtain favour of the LORD.
But he that sinneth against me wrongeth his own soul:
all they that hate me love death."

~ Proverbs 8:35-36

~~~~~~~~~~

These passages are but a glimpse into the Word of God on this subject.
You are encouraged to read the Holy Bible every day,
and walk in the light of His truth …
to grow your Faith.

Passages On
Avoiding Evil

~ †**†**† ~

"By mercy and truth iniquity is purged:
and by the fear of the LORD men depart from evil."

~ Proverbs 16:6

"Beloved, follow not that which is evil, but that which is good.
He that doeth good is of God:
but he that doeth evil hath not seen God."

~ 3 John 1:11

"As obedient children, not fashioning yourselves
according to the former lusts in your ignorance:
But as he which hath called you is holy,
so be ye holy in all manner of conversation;
Because it is written, Be ye holy; for I am holy."

~ 1 Peter 1:14-16

"Pray without ceasing.
In every thing give thanks:
for this is the will of God in Christ Jesus concerning you.
Quench not the Spirit.
Despise not prophesyings.
Prove all things; hold fast that which is good.
Abstain from all appearance of evil.

And the very God of peace sanctify you wholly;
and I pray God your whole spirit and soul and body be
preserved blameless unto the coming of our Lord Jesus Christ.

Faithful is he that calleth you, who also will do it."

~ 1 Thessalonians 5:17-24

"Deliver me, O my God, out of the hand of the wicked,
out of the hand of the unrighteous and cruel man."

~ Psalm 71:4

"Keep me from the snares which they have laid for me,
and the gins of the workers of iniquity."

~ Psalm 141:9

"Let love be without dissimulation.
Abhor that which is evil; cleave to that which is good."

~ Romans 12:9

"Be not overcome of evil, but overcome evil with good."

~ Romans 12:21

~~~~~~~~~~

These passages are but a glimpse into the Word of God on this subject.
You are encouraged to read the Holy Bible every day,
and walk in the light of His truth ...
to grow your Faith.

Passages On
Communication

"Let the words of my mouth, and the meditation of my heart,
be acceptable in thy sight, O LORD,
my strength, and my redeemer."

~ Psalm 19:14

"If any man speak, let him speak as the oracles of God; if any
man minister, let him do it as of the ability which God giveth:
that God in all things may be glorified through Jesus Christ,
to whom be praise and dominion for ever and ever."

~ 1 Peter 4:6

"Be not deceived:
evil communications corrupt good manners."

~ 1 Corinthians 15:33

"Blessings are upon the head of the just: but violence
covereth the mouth of the wicked."

~ Proverbs 10:6

"The mouth of a righteous man is a well of life: but violence
covereth the mouth of the wicked.
Hatred stirreth up strifes: but love covereth all sins."

~ Proverbs 10:11-12

"The words of the wicked are to lie in wait for blood:
but the mouth of the upright shall deliver them."

~ Proverbs 12:6

"A man shall be satisfied with good by the fruit of his mouth:
and the recompence of a
man's hands shall be rendered unto him."

~ Proverbs 12:14

"There is that speaketh like the piercings of a sword:
but the tongue of the wise is health."

~ Proverbs 12:18

"He that keepeth his mouth keepeth his life:
but he that openeth wide his lips shall have destruction."

~ Proverbs 13:3

"The heart of the righteous studieth to answer:
but the mouth of the wicked poureth out evil things."

~ Proverbs 15:28

"Even a fool, when he holdeth his peace,
is counted wise: and he that shutteth his lips
is esteemed a man of understanding."

~ Proverbs 17:28

"A man's belly shall be satisfied with the fruit of his mouth;
and with the increase of his lips shall he be filled.
Death and life are in the power of the tongue:
and they that love it shall eat the fruit thereof."

~ Proverbs 18:20-21

"Whoso keepeth his mouth and his tongue
keepeth his soul from troubles."

~ Proverbs 21:23

"Seest thou a man that is hasty in his words?
there is more hope of a fool than of him."

~ Proverbs 29:20

"Set a watch, O LORD, before my mouth;
keep the door of my lips."

~ Psalm 141:3

"For by thy words thou shalt be justified,
and by thy words thou shalt be condemned."

~ Matthew 12:37

"Thou hast proved mine heart; thou hast visited me in the
night; thou hast tried me, and shalt find nothing;
I am purposed that my mouth shall not transgress."

~ Psalm 17:3

"The LORD's voice crieth unto the city, and the man of wisdom
shall see thy name: hear ye the rod,
and who hath appointed it."

~ Micah 6:9

~~~~~~~~~~

These passages are but a glimpse into the Word of God on this subject.
You are encouraged to read the Holy Bible every day,
and walk in the light of His truth ...
to grow your Faith.

Passages On
Mercy & Forgiveness

"As far as the east is from the west,
so far hath he removed our transgressions from us."

~ Psalm 103:12

"To the Lord our God belong mercies and forgivenesses,
though we have rebelled against him;
Neither have we obeyed the voice of the LORD our God,
to walk in his laws,
which he set before us by his servants the prophets."

~ Daniel 9:9-10

"Blessed are the merciful: for they shall obtain mercy."

~ Matthew 5:7

"And forgive us our debts, as we forgive our debtors."

~ Matthew 6:12

"Then came Peter to him, and said, Lord, how oft shall my brother sin against me, and I forgive him? till seven times? Jesus saith unto him, I say not unto thee, Until seven times: but, Until seventy times seven."

~ Matthew 18:21-22

"Be ye therefore merciful, as your Father also is merciful. Judge not, and ye shall not be judged: condemn not, and ye shall not be condemned: forgive, and ye shall be forgiven: Give, and it shall be given unto you; good measure, pressed down, and shaken together, and running over, shall men give into your bosom. For with the same measure that ye mete withal it shall be measured to you again."

~ Luke 6:36-38

"And if he trespass against thee seven times in a day, and seven times in a day turn again to thee, saying, I repent; thou shalt forgive him."

~ Luke 17:4

"He hath shewed thee, O man, what is good; and what doth the LORD require of thee, but to do justly, and to love mercy, and to walk humbly with thy God?"

~ Micah 6:8

"And be ye kind one to another, tenderhearted, forgiving one another, even as God for Christ's sake hath forgiven you."

~ Ephesians 4:32

"Forbearing one another, and forgiving one another,
if any man have a quarrel against any:
even as Christ forgave you, so also do ye."

~ Colossians 3:13

"Knowing this, that our old man is crucified with him,
that the body of sin might be destroyed, that henceforth we
should not serve sin. For he that is dead is freed from sin."

~ Romans 6:6-7

"There is therefore now no condemnation to them which are
in Christ Jesus, who walk not after the flesh,
but after the Spirit.
For the law of the Spirit of life in Christ Jesus hath made me
free from the law of sin and death."

~ Romans 8:1-2

"Whereof the Holy Ghost also is a witness to us:
for after that he had said before,
This is the covenant that I will make with them after those
days, saith the Lord, I will put my laws into their hearts,
and in their minds will I write them;
And their sins and iniquities will I remember no more."

~ Hebrews 10:15-17

~~~~~~~~~~

These passages are but a glimpse into the Word of God on this subject.
You are encouraged to read the Holy Bible every day,
and walk in the light of His truth ...
to grow your Faith.

Passages On
Children

"Honour thy father and thy mother: that thy days may be long upon the land which the LORD thy God giveth thee."

~ Exodus 20:12

"Honour thy father and thy mother, as the Lord thy God hath commanded thee; that thy days may be prolonged, and that it may go well with thee, in the land which the Lord thy God giveth thee."

~ Deuteronomy 5:16

"Children, obey your parents in all things: for this is well pleasing unto the Lord."

~ Colossians 3:20

"My son, if sinners entice thee, consent thou not."

~ Proverbs 1:10

"Take fast hold of instruction; let her not go: keep her; for she is thy life."

~ Proverbs 4:13

"He that walketh with wise men shall be wise:
but a companion of fools shall be destroyed."

~ Proverbs 13:10

"Hear counsel, and receive instruction,
that thou mayest be wise in thy latter end."

~ Proverbs 19:20

"Whosoever therefore shall humble himself as this little child,
the same is greatest in the kingdom of heaven.
And whoso shall receive one such little child
in my name receiveth me."

~ Matthew 18:4-5

"The LORD by wisdom hath founded the earth;
by understanding hath he established the heavens.
By his knowledge the depths are broken up,
and the clouds drop down the dew.
My son, let not them depart from thine eyes:
keep sound wisdom and discretion:
So shall they be life unto thy soul, and grace to thy neck.
Then shalt thou walk in thy way safely,
and thy foot shall not stumble.
When thou liest down, thou shalt not be afraid:
yea, thou shalt lie down, and thy sleep shall be sweet."

~ Proverbs 3:19-24

"And they brought young children to him,
that he should touch them: and his disciples rebuked those
that brought them.
But when Jesus saw it, he was much displeased,
and said unto them,
Suffer the little children to come unto me, and forbid them
not: for of such is the kingdom of God."

~ Mark 10:13-14

"Hear thou, my son, and be wise,
and guide thine heart in the way."

~ Proverbs 23:19

"The LORD shall increase you more and more,
you and your children.
Ye are blessed of the LORD which made heaven and earth."

~ Psalm 115:14-15

"Lo, children are an heritage of the LORD:
and the fruit of the womb is his reward."

~ Psalm 127:3

~~~~~~~~~~

These passages are but a glimpse into the Word of God on this subject.
You are encouraged to read the Holy Bible every day,
and walk in the light of His truth …
to grow your Faith.

Passages On
Parenting

"Train up a child in the way he should go:
and when he is old, he will not depart from it."

~ Proverbs 22:6

"And, ye fathers, provoke not your children to wrath:
but bring them up in the nurture and
admonition of the Lord."

~ Ephesians 6:4

"The LORD shall increase you more and more,
you and your children.
Ye are blessed of the LORD which made heaven and earth."

~ Psalm 115:14-15

"Lo, children are an heritage of the LORD:
and the fruit of the womb is his reward."

~ Psalm 127:3

"Fathers, provoke not your children to anger,
lest they be discouraged."

~ Colossians 3:21

"Chasten thy son while there is hope,
and let not thy soul spare for his crying."

~ Proverbs 19:18

"The father of the righteous shall greatly rejoice: and he that
begetteth a wise child shall have joy of him."

~ Proverbs 23:24

"Correct thy son, and he shall give thee rest;
yea, he shall give delight unto thy soul."

~ Proverbs 29:17

~~~~~~~~~~

These passages are but a glimpse into the Word of God on this subject.
You are encouraged to read the Holy Bible every day,
and walk in the light of His truth …
to grow your Faith.

Passages On
Growing Old

"With the ancient is wisdom;
and in length of days understanding."

~ Job 12:12

"But speak thou the things which become sound doctrine:
That the aged men be sober, grave, temperate,
sound in faith, in charity, in patience.
The aged women likewise, that they be in behaviour as
becometh holiness, not false accusers, not given to much wine,
teachers of good things;
That they may teach the young women to be sober,
to love their husbands, to love their children,
To be discreet, chaste, keepers at home, good, obedient to their
own husbands, that the word of God be not blasphemed."

~ Titus 2:1-5

"The hoary head is a crown of glory,
if it be found in the way of righteousness."

~ Proverbs 16:31

"Children's children are the crown of old men;
and the glory of children are their fathers."

~ Proverbs 17:6

"The righteous shall flourish like the palm tree:
he shall grow like a cedar in Lebanon.
Those that be planted in the house of the LORD
shall flourish in the courts of our God."

~ Psalm 92:12-13

"Now also when I am old and greyheaded,
O God, forsake me not;
until I have shewed thy strength unto this generation,
and thy power to every one that is to come."

~ Psalm 71:18

~~~~~~~~~~

*These passages are but a glimpse into the Word of God on this subject.
You are encouraged to read the Holy Bible every day,
and walk in the light of His truth ...
to grow your Faith.*

Passages On
Anger

"Be not hasty in thy spirit to be angry:
for anger resteth in the bosom of fools."

~ Ecclesiastes 7:9

"Cease from anger, and forsake wrath:
fret not thyself in any wise to do evil."

~ Psalm 37:8

"Wherefore, my beloved brethren, let every man be swift to
hear, slow to speak, slow to wrath:
For the wrath of man worketh not the righteousness of God."

~ James 1:19-20

"Be ye angry, and sin not:
let not the sun go down upon your wrath:
Neither give place to the devil."

~ Ephesians 4:26-27

"I will therefore that men pray every where,
lifting up holy hands, without wrath and doubting."

~ 1 Timothy 2:8

"Stand in awe, and sin not:
commune with your own heart upon your bed, and be still."

~ Psalm 4:4

"He that is soon angry dealeth foolishly:
and a man of wicked devices is hated."

~ Proverbs 14:17

"A wrathful man stirreth up strife:
but he that is slow to anger appeaseth strife."

~ Proverbs 15:18

"A violent man enticeth his neighbour,
and leadeth him into the way that is not good."

~ Proverbs 16:29

"Make no friendship with an angry man;
and with a furious man thou shalt not go:
Lest thou learn his ways, and get a snare to thy soul."

~ Proverbs 22:24-25

"Scornful men bring a city into a snare:
but wise men turn away wrath."

~ Proverbs 29:8

~~~~~~~~~

These passages are but a glimpse into the Word of God on this subject.
You are encouraged to read the Holy Bible every day,
and walk in the light of His truth ...
to grow your Faith.

Passages On
Loneliness

"Draw nigh to God, and he will draw nigh to you."

~ James 4:8

"As the mountains are round about Jerusalem,
so the LORD is round about his people
from henceforth even for ever."

~ Psalm 125:2

"The LORD is nigh unto all them that call upon him,
to all that call upon him in truth."

~ Psalm 145:18

"For none of us liveth to himself,
and no man dieth to himself."

~ Romans 14:7

"Let your conversation be without covetousness;
and be content with such things as ye have:
for he hath said, I will never leave thee, nor forsake thee."

~ Hebrews 13:5

"Let not your heart be troubled:
ye believe in God, believe also in me.
In my Father's house are many mansions:
if it were not so, I would have told you.
I go to prepare a place for you.
And if I go and prepare a place for you,
I will come again, and receive you unto myself;
that where I am, there ye may be also."

~ John 14:1-3

"If ye love me, keep my commandments.
And I will pray the Father, a
nd he shall give you another Comforter,
that he may abide with you for ever;
Even the Spirit of truth; whom the world cannot receive,
because it seeth him not, neither knoweth him:
but ye know him; for he dwelleth with you,
and shall be in you."

~ John 14:15-17

"Jesus answered and said unto him, If a man love me,
he will keep my words: and my Father will love him, and we
will come unto him, and make our abode with him."

~ John 14:23

"God setteth the solitary in families:
he bringeth out those which are bound with chains:
but the rebellious dwell in a dry land."

~ Psalm 68:6

"Teaching them to observe all things whatsoever I have commanded you: and, lo, I am with you always, even unto the end of the world. Amen."

~ Matthew 18:20

~~~~~~~~~~

These passages are but a glimpse into the Word of God on this subject.
You are encouraged to read the Holy Bible every day,
and walk in the light of His truth ...
to grow your Faith.

Passages On
Sleep & Peace

"I will both lay me down in peace, and sleep:
for thou, LORD, only makest me dwell in safety."

~ Psalm 4:8

"Be anxious for nothing,
but in everything by prayer and supplication with
thanksgiving let your requests be made known to God.
And the peace of God, which surpasses all comprehension,
will guard your hearts and your minds in Christ Jesus."

~ Philippians 4:6-7, NASB

"I will bless the LORD, who hath given me counsel:
my reins also instruct me in the night seasons."

~ Psalm 16:7

"The LORD will give strength unto his people;
the LORD will bless his people with peace."

~ Psalm 29:11

"Great peace have they which love thy law:
and nothing shall offend them."

~ Psalm 119:165

"It is vain for you to rise up early, to sit up late,
to eat the bread of sorrows:
for so he giveth his beloved sleep."

~ Psalm 127:2

"Peace I leave with you, my peace I give unto you:
not as the world giveth, give I unto you.
Let not your heart be troubled, neither let it be afraid."

~ John 14:27

"These things I have spoken unto you, that in me ye might
have peace. In the world ye shall have tribulation:
but be of good cheer; I have overcome the world."

~ John 16:33

"O that thou hadst hearkened to my commandments!
then had thy peace been as a river,
and thy righteousness as the waves of the sea."

~ Isaiah 48:18

"Glory to God in the highest,
and on earth peace, good will toward men."

~ Luke 2:14

"And let the peace of God rule in your hearts,
to the which also ye are called in one body;
and be ye thankful."

~ Colossians 3:15

"Now the Lord of peace himself give you peace always by all
means. The Lord be with you all."

~ 2 Thessalonians 3:16

~~~~~~~~~~

These passages are but a glimpse into the Word of God on this subject.
You are encouraged to read the Holy Bible every day,
and walk in the light of His truth …
to grow your Faith.

Passages On
Gossip

"A talebearer revealeth secrets:
but he that is of a faithful spirit concealeth the matter."

~ Proverbs 11:13

"A wicked doer giveth heed to false lips;
and a liar giveth ear to a naughty tongue."

~ Proverbs 17:4

"The words of a talebearer are as wounds,
and they go down into the innermost parts of the belly."

~ Proverbs 18:8

"An ungodly witness scorneth judgment:
and the mouth of the wicked devoureth iniquity."

~ Proverbs 19:28

"He that goeth about as a talebearer revealeth secrets:
therefore meddle not with him that flattereth with his lips."

~ Proverbs 20:19

"Where no wood is, there the fire goeth out:
so where there is no talebearer, the strife ceaseth."

~ Proverbs 26:20

"Thou shalt not raise a false report:
put not thine hand with the wicked
to be an unrighteous witness."

~ Exodus 23:1

"Well reported of for good works;
if she have brought up children,
if she have lodged strangers,
if she have washed the saints' feet,
if she have relieved the afflicted,
if she have diligently followed every good work.
But the younger widows refuse: for when they have begun
to wax wanton against Christ, they will marry;
Having damnation, because they have cast off their first faith.
And withal they learn to be idle, wandering about from
house to house; and not only idle, but tattlers also and
busybodies, speaking things which they ought not.
I will therefore that the younger women marry,
bear children, guide the house, give none occasion
to the adversary to speak reproachfully.
For some are already turned aside after Satan."

~ 1 Timothy 5:10-15

"But I say unto you,
That every idle word that men shall speak,
they shall give account thereof in the day of judgment.
For by thy words thou shalt be justified,
and by thy words thou shalt be condemned."

~ Matthew 12:36-37

~~~~~~~~~~

*These passages are but a glimpse into the Word of God on this subject.
You are encouraged to read the Holy Bible every day,
and walk in the light of His truth …
to grow your Faith.*

Passages On
Money & Wealth

"But godliness with contentment is great gain.
For we brought nothing into this world,
and it is certain we can carry nothing out.
And having food and raiment let us be therewith content.
But they that will be rich fall into temptation and a snare,
and into many foolish and hurtful lusts,
which drown men in destruction and perdition.
For the love of money is the root of all evil:
which while some coveted after, they have erred from the
faith, and pierced themselves through with many sorrows."

~ 1 Timothy 6:6-10

"He that loveth silver shall not be satisfied with silver;
nor he that loveth abundance with increase:
this is also vanity."

~ Ecclesiastes 5:10

"There is that scattereth, and yet increaseth; and there is that
withholdeth more than is meet, but it tendeth to poverty.
The liberal soul shall be made fat:
and he that watereth shall be watered also himself."

~ Proverbs 11:24-25

"Honour the LORD with thy substance,
and with the firstfruits of all thine increase:
So shall thy barns be filled with plenty,
and thy presses shall burst out with new wine."

~ Proverbs 3:9-10

"Distributing to the necessity of saints;
given to hospitality."

~ Romans 12:13

"Every man according as he purposeth in his heart,
so let him give; not grudgingly, or of necessity:
for God loveth a cheerful giver."

~ 2 Corinthians 9:7

"I have shewed you all things, how that so labouring ye ought
to support the weak, and to remember the words of the Lord
Jesus, how he said, It is more blessed to give than to receive."

~ Acts 20:35

~~~~~~~~~~

These passages are but a glimpse into the Word of God on this subject.
You are encouraged to read the Holy Bible every day,
and walk in the light of His truth ...
to grow your Faith.

Passages On
Work

"In all labour there is profit:
but the talk of the lips tendeth only to penury."

~ Proverbs 14:23

"Whether therefore ye eat, or drink, or whatsoever ye do,
do all to the glory of God."

~ Psalm 37:23

"And whatsoever ye do, do it heartily,
as to the Lord, and not unto men;
Knowing that of the Lord ye shall receive the reward
of the inheritance: for ye serve the Lord Christ."

~ Colossians 3:23-24

"But let every man prove his own work, and then shall he
have rejoicing in himself alone, and not in another.
For every man shall bear his own burden."

~ Galatians 6:4-5

"Labour not for the meat which perisheth, but for that meat which endureth unto everlasting life, which the Son of man shall give unto you: for him hath God the Father sealed."

~ John 6:27

"I must work the works of him that sent me, while it is day: the night cometh, when no man can work."

~ John 9:4

"And there are diversities of operations, but it is the same God which worketh all in all."

~ 1 Corinthians 12:6

"He that tilleth his land shall be satisfied with bread: but he that followeth vain persons is void of understanding."

~ Proverbs 12:11

"He also that is slothful in his work is brother to him that is a great waster."

~ Proverbs 18:9

"Labour not to be rich: cease from thine own wisdom."

~ Proverbs 23:4

~~~~~~~~~~

These passages are but a glimpse into the Word of God on this subject.
You are encouraged to read the Holy Bible every day,
and walk in the light of His truth …
to grow your Faith.

Passages On
Poverty

"Therefore I say unto you, Take no thought for your life, what
ye shall eat, or what ye shall drink; nor yet for your body,
what ye shall put on. Is not the life more than meat,
and the body than raiment?"

~ Matthew 6:25

"Better is little with the fear of the LORD
than great treasure and trouble therewith."

~ Proverbs 15:16

"Better is the poor that walketh in his uprightness,
than he that is perverse in his ways, though he be rich."

~ Proverbs 28:6

"For thou hast been a strength to the poor, a strength to the
needy in his distress, a refuge from the storm, a shadow from
the heat, when the blast of the terrible ones
is as a storm against the wall."

~ Isaiah 25:4

"The righteous considereth the cause of the poor:
but the wicked regardeth not to know it."

~ Proverbs 29:7

"I know that the LORD will maintain the cause of the afflicted,
and the right of the poor."

~ Psalm 140:12

"Remove far from me vanity and lies: give me neither poverty
nor riches; feed me with food convenient for me:
Lest I be full, and deny thee, and say, Who is the LORD?
or lest I be poor, and steal,
and take the name of my God in vain."

~ Proverbs 30:8-9

"Open thy mouth for the dumb
in the cause of all such as are appointed to destruction.
Open thy mouth, judge righteously,
and plead the cause of the poor and needy."

~ Proverbs 31:8-9

"The LORD is my shepherd; I shall not want."

~ Psalm 23:1

~~~~~~~~~~

These passages are but a glimpse into the Word of God on this subject.
You are encouraged to read the Holy Bible every day,
and walk in the light of His truth ...
to grow your Faith.

Passages On
Laziness

"That ye be not slothful, but followers of them who through
faith and patience inherit the promises."

~ Hebrews 6:12

"How long wilt thou sleep, O sluggard?
when wilt thou arise out of thy sleep?
Yet a little sleep, a little slumber,
a little folding of the hands to sleep:
So shall thy poverty come as one that travelleth,
and thy want as an armed man."

~ Proverbs 6:9-11

"Slothfulness casteth into a deep sleep;
and an idle soul shall suffer hunger."

~ Proverbs 19:15

"For even when we were with you, this we commanded you,
that if any would not work, neither should he eat."

~ 2 Thessalonians 3:10

"He becometh poor that dealeth with a slack hand:
but the hand of the diligent maketh rich."
~ Proverbs 10:4

"Now we command you, brethren, in the name of our Lord
Jesus Christ, that ye withdraw yourselves from
every brother that walketh disorderly,
and not after the tradition which he received of us."

~ 2 Thessalonians 3:6

~~~~~~~~~~

These passages are but a glimpse into the Word of God on this subject.
You are encouraged to read the Holy Bible every day,
and walk in the light of His truth ...
to grow your Faith.

Passages On
Grief & Sorrow

"For godly sorrow worketh repentance to salvation not to be repented of: but the sorrow of the world worketh death."

~ 2 Corinthians 7:10

"The LORD is nigh unto them that are of a broken heart; and saveth such as be of a contrite spirit."

~ Psalm 34:18

"Why art thou cast down, O my soul? and why art thou disquieted within me? hope in God: for I shall yet praise him, who is the health of my countenance, and my God."

~ Psalm 43:5

"My soul melteth for heaviness: strengthen thou me according unto thy word."

~ Psalm 119:28

"He healeth the broken in heart, and bindeth up their wounds."

~ Psalm 147:3

"Rejoice with them that do rejoice,
and weep with them that weep."

~ Romans 12:15

"Blessed are ye that weep now: for ye shall laugh."

~ Luke 6:21

"Jesus wept."

~ John 11:35

"Then saith He unto them, My soul is exceeding sorrowful,
even unto death: tarry ye here, and watch with me."

~ Matthew 26:38

"And the ransomed of the LORD shall return, and come to
Zion with songs and everlasting joy upon their heads:
they shall obtain joy and gladness,
and sorrow and sighing shall flee away."

~ Isaiah 35:10

"Surely he hath borne our griefs, and carried our sorrows:
yet we did esteem him stricken, smitten of God, and afflicted."

~ Isaiah 53:4

"He will swallow up death in victory; and the Lord GOD will wipe away tears from off all faces; and the rebuke of his people shall he take away from off all the earth: for the LORD hath spoken it."

~ Isaiah 25:8

~~~~~~~~~~

These passages are but a glimpse into the Word of God on this subject.
You are encouraged to read the Holy Bible every day,
and walk in the light of His truth ...
to grow your Faith.

Passages On
Spiritual Gifts

"For I would that all men were even as I myself.
But every man hath his proper gift of God,
one after this manner, and another after that."

~ 1 Corinthians 7:7

"Now there are diversities of gifts, but the same Spirit."

~ 1 Corinthians 12:4

"But the manifestation of the Spirit
is given to every man to profit withal.
For to one is given by the Spirit the word of wisdom;
to another the word of knowledge by the same Spirit;
To another faith by the same Spirit;
to another the gifts of healing by the same Spirit;
To another the working of miracles; to another prophecy;
to another discerning of spirits; to another divers kinds of
tongues; to another the interpretation of tongues:
But all these worketh that one and the selfsame Spirit,
dividing to every man severally as he will."

~ 1 Corinthians 12:7-11

"So we, being many, are one body in Christ,
and every one members one of another.

Having then gifts differing according to the grace
that is given to us, whether prophecy,
let us prophesy according to the proportion of faith;
Or ministry, let us wait on our ministering:
or he that teacheth, on teaching;
Or he that exhorteth, on exhortation: he that giveth,
let him do it with simplicity; he that ruleth, with diligence;
he that sheweth mercy, with cheerfulness.
Let love be without dissimulation. Abhor that which is evil;
cleave to that which is good."

~ Romans 12:5-9

"And he gave some, apostles; and some, prophets;
and some, evangelists; and some, pastors and teachers;
For the perfecting of the saints, for the work of the ministry,
for the edifying of the body of Christ:
Till we all come in the unity of the faith,
and of the knowledge of the Son of God, unto a perfect man,
unto the measure of the stature of the fullness of Christ:
That we henceforth be no more children, tossed to and fro,
and carried about with every wind of doctrine, by the sleight
of men, and cunning craftiness,
whereby they lie in wait to deceive;
But speaking the truth in love, may grow up into him in all
things, which is the head, even Christ:
From whom the whole body fitly joined together and
compacted by that which every joint supplieth,
according to the effectual working in
the measure of every part,
maketh increase of the body unto
the edifying of itself in love."

~ Ephesians 4:11-16

"As every man hath received the gift,
even so minister the same one to another,
as good stewards of the manifold grace of God."

~ 1 Peter 4:10

~~~~~~~~~~

These passages are but a glimpse into the Word of God on this subject.
You are encouraged to read the Holy Bible every day,
and walk in the light of His truth …
to grow your Faith.

Passages On
Help

~ †✝† ~

"Fear thou not; for I am with thee: be not dismayed; for I am
thy God: I will strengthen thee; yea, I will help thee; yea,
I will uphold thee with the right hand of my righteousness.
Behold, all they that were incensed against thee shall be
ashamed and confounded: they shall be as nothing;
and they that strive with thee shall perish.
Thou shalt seek them, and shalt not find them, even them that
contended with thee: they that war against thee shall be as
nothing, and as a thing of nought.
For I the LORD thy God will hold thy right hand,
saying unto thee, Fear not; I will help thee."

~ Isaiah 41:10-13

"I will lift up mine eyes unto the hills,
from whence cometh my help.
My help cometh from the LORD,
which made heaven and earth."

~ Psalm 121:1-2

"The Lord knoweth how to deliver the godly out of
temptations, and to reserve the unjust unto the day of
judgment to be punished:

But chiefly them that walk after the flesh in the lust of
uncleanness, and despise government.
Presumptuous are they,
selfwilled, they are not afraid to speak evil of dignities."

~ 2 Peter 2:9-10

"But my God shall supply all your need
According to his riches in glory by Christ Jesus."

~ Philippians 4:19

"Trust in the LORD with all thine heart;
and lean not unto thine own understanding.
In all thy ways acknowledge him,
and he shall direct thy paths."

~ Proverbs 3:5-6

"And all things, whatsoever ye shall ask in prayer,
believing, ye shall receive."

~Matthew 21:22

"Help me, O LORD my God:
O save me according to thy mercy:
That they may know that this is thy hand;
that thou, LORD, hast done it."

~ Psalm 109:26-27

"Therefore I say unto you, Take no thought for your life,
what ye shall eat, or what ye shall drink; nor yet for your
body, what ye shall put on. Is not the life more than meat,

and the body than raiment?
Behold the fowls of the air: for they sow not,
neither do they reap, nor gather into barns; yet your heavenly
Father feedeth them. Are ye not much better than they?
Which of you by taking thought can add
one cubit unto his stature?
And why take ye thought for raiment? Consider the lilies of
the field, how they grow; they toil not, neither do they spin:
And yet I say unto you, That even Solomon in all his glory
was not arrayed like one of these.
Wherefore, if God so clothe the grass of the field,
which to day is, and to morrow is cast into the oven,
shall he not much more clothe you, O ye of little faith?
Therefore take no thought, saying, What shall we eat? or,
What shall we drink? or, Wherewithal shall we be clothed?
(For after all these things do the Gentiles seek:) for your
heavenly Father knoweth that ye have need of all these things.
But seek ye first the kingdom of God, and his righteousness;
and all these things shall be added unto you."

~ Matthew 6:25-33

"The LORD preserveth the simple:
I was brought low, and he helped me."

~ Psalm 116:6

"Be anxious for nothing,
but in everything by prayer and supplication with
thanksgiving let your requests be made known to God.
And the peace of God, which surpasses all comprehension,
will guard your hearts and your minds in Christ Jesus."

~ Philippians 4:6-7, NASB

~~~~~~~~~~

These passages are but a glimpse into the Word of God on this subject.
You are encouraged to read the Holy Bible every day,
and walk in the light of His truth ...
to grow your Faith.

Afterword

Shining His Light

"Let your light so shine before men, that they may see your good works, and glorify your Father which is in heaven."

~ Matthew 5:16

Always remember YOU are here for a purpose, and that purpose is to glorify God and do good. As our faith grows, so must our efforts to do good. As the Book of James observes, *"Even so faith, if it hath not works, is dead, being alone."*[161] And the Word goes on to state, *"For as the body without the spirit is dead, so faith without works is dead also."*[162]

Know that you and I were born for a time such as this! A time of great responsibility to be greatly borne, a time when we renew our faith and our hope, and embrace the promises of God. A time of dedicating or rededicating to studying and meditating on the Word of God, so we might have a more personal and intimate relationship with Him. A time when we might fully realize God's personal plan for our particular lives, and we might carry the banner of the great crusade ... and do good, all to His glory!

King Solomon, arguably the wisest man of the Old

---

[161] James 2:17.
[162] James 2:26.

Testament, gave us the benefit of his lifelong journey, a life of trial and triumph, studying and meditating on Holy Scripture, a life of learning and walking with God. Solomon gave us the benefit of what he ultimately learned in his lifelong journey, and he shares it with us in Ecclesiastes 12:13, *"Let us hear the conclusion of the whole matter: Fear God, and keep his commandments: for this is the whole duty of man."*

Remember, too, you and I are commissioned by God. In Mark 16:15, we read His great commandment:

> And He said unto them, Go ye into all the world, and preach the gospel to every creature.

Are you ready to accept that Commission? I hope so! And while you contemplate that question, consider beginning your journey by helping others already in the battle. In this regard, I speak of helping out at your local Bible-believing church, or donating to the good works of those I mentioned at the very beginning of this book in the Dedication. I am speaking of Paul and Vickie Hafer of St. Marys, Georgia. These two saints followed God's calling and began a powerful ministry for the glory of Christ. Their ministry is Lighthouse Christian Broadcasting, *"The Lighthouse"* WECC Christian Radio Station.

In the words of Paul Hafer, *"Ever since 1985, God had been faithful to provide for our little 2,000 watt, daytime-only Christian radio station on AM 1190, and we strived to be faithful stewards. Then in 2002, with the prayer and partnership of WECC listeners and supporters, God greatly increased our opportunity to minister, with a 16,000 watt, 24 hour, FM station! Now, more than 12 years later, with 30,000 watts on FM 89.3, reaching listeners around the world streaming on the internet at TheLighthouseFM.org, and still on AM 1190, our mission continues, to Share His Story, and Shine His Light, at The Lighthouse WECC!"*

But The Lighthouse is more than *"a Christian radio station"* that serves a listening audience in southeast Georgia and northeast Florida, it is a full-service Christian ministry with a mission to spread the Good News of Jesus Christ ...

- To encourage Faith in Believers with God's Word in Music, Teaching, and Testimony.
- To point unbelievers to the Gospel of our Savior & Lord Jesus Christ.
- To provide programs and Ministry opportunities that unite and strengthen the entire Body of Christ.

Lighthouse Christian Broadcasting, *"The Lighthouse"* WECC, is a multi-faceted, interdenominational non-profit mission established to encourage people to walk by faith in God, by hearing His Word. By the light of His Word, we have hope and joy for an abundant life and future, in order to carry out our mission, to be the light of the world!

This Interdenominational ministry includes:

- A Christian radio ministry on 89.3 FM in southeast Georgia and northeast Florida, and around the world on the internet at TheLighthouseFM.org.
- The Rock Ministry for Youth.
- Ladies Bible Study.
- Men's Prayer Meeting.
- Intercessory Prayer for our families, our communities, and our nation.
- And much, much more!

Both Paul and Vickie Hafer, my friends, say, *"Our purpose at Lighthouse Christian Broadcasting is to promote unity in the Body of Christ, in order to enjoy fellowship and worship together, that we might also better encourage and build up one another, and accomplish the great commission of our Lord Jesus Christ."*

The Lighthouse truly does shine a light ... His Light! It points the way to living life with Faith and His power, dwelling on good things, and with the virtues of faith, hope and love at the forefront. This is what *"The Lighthouse"* is all about, the story of what a small group of Spirit-filled saints sharing the Good News of Jesus Christ can do! The Lighthouse points the way to Truth, and in that Truth, an anchor that grounds us to an immovable foundation.

That foundation of *"The Lighthouse"* is the rock upon which Jesus spoke to His disciples in Matthew16:18. It is the absolute Faith that Jesus Christ is Lord, and He is the same yesterday, today, and forever,[163] and He loves YOU![164]

---

[163] Hebrews 13:8.

The primary Lighthouse Keepers are Paul and Vickie Hafer. And like the traditional lighthouse keepers of old, they toil day and night to keep the light shining bright. Through every season and circumstance, they and their Lighthouse team do the day to day work that needs to be done to keep His light shining.

And YOU, like me, can be a *"Lighthouse Keeper"* and a member of their team, too! Go online at TheLighthouseFM.org and make a generous donation to this great and good work! This would be doing good for others and the cause of Christ! Sign up to donate on a monthly basis, or send a donation to keep His Light shining through this wonderful ministry! Please do it TODAY, and send me an email telling me about your good work! These are the stories of the power of Christ in us that true lift each other, our families, our communities, and our nation! Be a part of this godly effort!

Let your faith be accompanied by the power of God to do good! As Jesus said, *"Let your light so shine before men, that they may see your good works, and glorify your Father which is in heaven."*[165] This is living the Great Commission!

Surrender to the Lord and live a life of substance and meaning, for this is the whole duty of man.

Amen.

~~~~~~~~~~

---

[164] John 3:16.
[165] Matthew 5:16.

"In the beginning was the Word,
and the Word was with God, and the Word was God."
~ John 1:1

About the Author

Judge Hal Moroz

Whether therefore ye eat, or drink, or whatsoever ye do, do all to the glory of God.

~ Psalm 37:23

Judge Hal Moroz is an Attorney and Counselor at Law, who served as an Assistant District Attorney, a County Judge, and a city Chief Judge in the great State of Georgia. His practice in the law has ranged from prosecuting criminals on behalf of the State of Georgia to representing American military veterans in courts up to and including the Supreme Court of the United States.

Judge Moroz is also an accomplished soldier and statesman, as well as a retired U.S. Army officer, having served in the Airborne Infantry. Judge Moroz served on the faculty of Florida Coastal School of Law in Jacksonville,

Florida, and the State Bar of Georgia's Institute for Continuing Legal Education (ICLE) in the education of attorneys. He is a former candidate for the U.S. Congress, and served as Special Counsel to the Georgia Republican Party's First Congressional District Committee in the 2000 primary and general elections.

Hal Moroz is also a news and political commentator, sharing his insight of the law and politics on a variety of popular media programs. He is also a prolific writer, having authored numerous legal articles, weekly legal newspaper columns, and books. Copies of his many books can be ordered at Amazon.com or any major online bookstore!

Hal Moroz can be reached through an internet search
or through his email at: hal@morozlaw.com or his website:
MorozLaw.com

I am an American who lives in the shadow of the Cross ...

I walk humbly before God,
I stand tall before men,
And I stand in the gap for the cause of Christ and America!

~ Judge Hal Moroz

Other Books by
Hal Moroz

- **The Making of a Supreme Court Justice**
- **It's Morning Again in America**
- **Armor of the Republic**
- **Resurrecting Lee**
- **5 Things Every Veteran Needs to Know**
- **The Road Less Travelled**
- **Faith to Move Mountains**
- **Resurrecting Jesus**
- **Veterans Law & Benefits**
- **Re-Discovering Ronald Reagan**
- **Resurrecting Lincoln**
- **Resurrecting Kennedy**
- **Resurrecting Reagan**
- **Living a Godly Life**
- **Federal Benefits for Veterans, Dependents and Survivors**
- **President Ronald Reagan: Let's Make America Great Again!**
- **A Christmas Carol** *(by Charles Dickens with a special Introduction by Hal Moroz)*
- **The Rough Riders** *(by Theodore Roosevelt with a sp;ecial Introduction by Hal Moroz)*
- **And Many More** *(Search for books by Hal Moroz at Amazon.com or any major online bookstore)*

ORDER YOUR COPIES TODAY!

Made in the USA
Middletown, DE
05 October 2022

12008300R00142